From Abram To Abraham

Flying Eagle Publications

Unless otherwise noted, all Scripture King James Version of the Bible. Public Domain.

Scripture marked WEB is taken from World English Bible. Public Domain.

"Scripture taken from the Literal Translation of the Holy Bible Copyright © 1976 - 2000
By Jay P. Green, Sr.
Used by permission of the copyright holder."

From Abram To Abraham
ISBN:978-17327688-1-9

Flying Eagle Publications.com

Editors Dee Farrell and Jessica Kruger.
Illustration: Haley Jula.
Cover Image: Eddie and Carolina Stigson courtesy of Unsplash.

©2019 Flying Eagle Publications. All Rights Reserved under International Copyright Law. No part of this book may be reproduced or transmitted in any form by any means.

Printed in the United States.

The Bible is not a book about psychology even though it deals with your deepest desires and matters of your heart. It is not a book about finance even though it talks about money— a lot. It is not a medical book but it describes people who were healed of various conditions.

It is not a science book even though it reveals scientific things. It is not strictly a history book either just because it is the definitive guide to the past. So what is it?

When you turn the pages of the Bible you meet the God who created you. He tells you why and the thoughts He thinks about you, what He has done for you and how He hopes you will respond.

The Bible at its purest essence is the message of a doting, loving Father to His child. He sits you down and shows you the world He has provided for you. He wants you to know how it works because He's given it to you. You are now the caretaker of His creation. He's given His authority to you.

One day He'll return, He tells you, but for now it is yours. But be careful. There is an invisible enemy. Follow the established rules of My kingdom, God advises, use the fixed principles, and the enemy won't defeat you.

Abraham had to learn these things. Before there was a Bible. He was a man like any other. Common. Ordinary. But his life was not.

His story may seem heavy with myth and legend. Like the ancient temples he saw, his treasure was buried by our more modern revelations and whims. But men and women are blowing off the dust, taking another look and discovering a world they didn't know existed.

Matthew J. Adams said, "We used to think that EB I society in general was not complex enough for political and social hierarchies, but the Great Temple and the settlement at Tel Megiddo East are changing that."

We can be grateful to Adams and archaeologists like Bryant G. Wood and his work at The Associates For Biblical Research for showing us this world. Wood is known for his work identifying Jericho with the Israelite Conquest of Canaan and his investigations at Sodom and Numeira.

But there are many others; men and women whose research is pointing to a bigger picture than anyone believed possible.

Abraham got more than a glimpse of that picture. He lived the adventure.

∼ The Editors

As ye have therefore received Christ Jesus the Lord, so walk ye in him: Rooted and built up in him, and stablished in the faith, as ye have been taught, abounding therein with thanksgiving. Beware lest any man spoil you through philosophy and vain deceit, after the tradition of men, after the rudiments of the world, and not after Christ.

Col 2:6-8

Abraham

Chapter 1
Of Names and Family

You might not think about this, but every people group throughout time has named their children.[1] What that name meant to a child, however, depended on the culture.

It depends even today. For example, if you live in the Philippines, your name can change as you grow older. In Mongolia, people stop calling you by your name when you are an adult. Instead, they refer to you as woman or man or old woman or old man. You wouldn't be offended either because it is considered disrespectful to say a grown person's name. In some cultures like the Inuit or Japanese, your name is what gives you your soul.[2]

Did you know that in France, you might live next to someone for years and never know their first name? And you shouldn't ask. It is considered rude to ask such a personal question. It may be considered brazen to offer your first name too soon. Naming a baby is also serious business in American culture, but it is not so much about giving the child a soul as giving them a name that makes them stand out from others, which happens to be an American thing.

---

[1] Onomastics (AHnaMASticks) is the study of personal names.
[2] Ellen S. Bramwell, "Personal Names and Anthropology," *Oxford Handbook of Names* (Oxford:Oxford University Press, 2016) 18.3.2- 18.3.3.

Abram's father, Terah, knew the importance of names. He knew God placed great importance on them, and he believed that a name would determine the character and the destiny of his son. Rabbi Benjamin Blech says names are "The story of our spiritual potential as well as our life's mission."[3] He reminds us when God created the world, God spoke words, names for things that became substance and gave the substance an identity and purpose.

In the same way, our names have power to create and define us. Not only do they help us form an opinion of ourselves, but they cause others to form an attitude towards us as well, such as potential friends, teachers and employers.

Shakespeare said any name is sweet. But that is not a Hebrew thought. It is not God's either. Names have meaning. There are people in the Bible who became what they were named: Noah, rest; Nabal, fool; Hannah, favor and grace; Leah the mother of six sons, weary.

Terah chose the name Abram which means exalted father. It was a good name. It carried the idea of nobility, dignity and being joyful or extremely happy. Terah set the boundaries for his son's life and proclaimed Abram would be a noble, dignified, extremely happy father.

Except he wasn't. Abram had married a woman who couldn't have children. Genesis 11:29-30 says, "... the name of Abram's wife was Sarai... But Sarai was barren; she had no child."

In his defense, Terah didn't know Sarai couldn't have children when he picked a wife for his son. But that never caused Abram to change his name. He never changed his purpose either. Being a father, having a son, was all he wanted.

God understood Abram's desire. Every man needed an heir, some-

---

[3] Rabbi Benjamin Blech, "Judaism & the Power of Names," Apr 20, 2013, aish.com.

one to carry on their name. God wanted to give him a son. But He had a bigger life purpose planned for Abram than Abram realized.

Abram's obedience and disobedience in living out his purpose made him famous. You might already know Abram is Abraham, the father of the Jewish people. He is also an ancestor of Jesus.

To start His plan for Abram in motion, God sent him on a journey. Later, Abram became Abraham which means the father of many nations. Abram had to learn how to be made right with God, but his struggle to believe encourages and teaches Christians around the world.

In this book we will follow Abram's personal journey to become Abraham, the man who teaches us how to have faith in God. Abraham is known today as the father of three cultures and two religions. But that is only part of his story. Let's begin by finding out more about his family and where they first lived.

Abraham was called a Hebrew. But what is a Hebrew?

The word habiru was first found in Sumerian literature during the reign of a king named Shulgi. Habiru is also spelled *habiri* and as *habbatu* in the Akkadian language. The word is translated as brigand or a highway robber. A brigand is a member of a gang who robs someone. You can see then that a habiru was not a person with a good reputation. Was Abraham a highway robber? No; keep reading.

The Sumerian inscriptions described a habiru as a person who was destructive, independent and rebellious who lived in tents away from the towns. Sumerian kings hired them for military campaigns, but they were never part of a regular army. The kings paid them with clothing and livestock which must have been what they wanted, and even though their services were probably appreciated, the habiru remained separate from the townspeople. That might have been appreciated too. Their way of life continued well after the Sumerian Empire fell.

From the inscriptions, it seems the word habiru identified a group of people from a social standpoint instead of a specific family or ethnic group. The habiru were a people who remained aloof from the culture and cities around them; they were sometimes dangerous criminals and sometimes helpful soldiers to kings.

The Amarna Tablets say the habiru invaded Canaan, leveling the cities and destroying them. This is a reference to Abraham's descendants, Joshua and the Israelites when they left the wilderness to take over the Promised Land.

You might think habiru is an ancient variation of the word Hebrew. The Hebrews of the Old Testament did live in tents. Abraham lived in a tent. Hebrews did separate themselves from societies that worshipped idols. Abraham separated himself from Canaanite culture. The Hebrews under Joshua did invade Canaan and destroy cities. They also fought in wars. Abraham fought in a war, and it was his descendents who conquered Canaan.

Many people living in Canaan during the time of Joshua's wars probably did think of Abraham's Hebrew family as outlaws. The Amarna Tablets were letters written by Canaanite kings and sent to Egyptian or Hyksos pharaohs pleading desperately for help against invaders. Here is a portion of the inscription on an Amarna Tablet from ruler Abdu-Heba of Jerusalem:

> So certain as the king, my Lord, lives, when the commissioners come, I will say: 'Lost are the territories of the king. Do you not hear to me? All the rulers are lost; the king, my Lord, does not have a single ruler left.' May the king direct his attention to the archers, and may the king, my Lord, send troops of archers, the king has no more lands. The

Hapiru sack the territories of the king. If there are archers (here) this year, all the territories of the king will remain (intact); but if there are no archers, the territories of the king, my Lord, will be lost! [4]

Hapiru is another spelling of habiru. Scholars say they do not know for sure if habiru is a word for Hebrew, and all that can be said is habiru was a general word for people of a certain type. But they know there are similarities between the two groups in some situations. In inscriptions like the one above the word habiru is confidently associated with the Hebrews, especially during the takeover of Canaan.

How did God use the word Hebrew? The first time we read the word Hebrew in the Bible, it is used to describe Abraham. "And one who had escaped came and told Abram the Hebrew; for he was living among the oaks of Mamre the Amorite." (Genesis 14:13) So, we learn that Abraham was called a Hebrew and was living in Mamre which is Hebron.[5] The word used for Hebrew is *'ibrîy (ivREE)*. It means an Eberite or a descendant of Eber, one from beyond. Both of these meanings applied to Abraham.

In Genesis 10, Eber (Ayvair) is a grandson of Shem and an ancestor of Abraham. *'Êbêr* means the region beyond or on the other side, to cross over or pass through. Genesis 10:21 says Shem was the father of all Eber's children who lived in the region beyond. Many scholars assume Eber crossed to the west bank of the Euphrates River. We know at some point, after the Tower of Babel, Eber crossed over something and settled *there*. We will talk about where *there* might be later.

Abraham also crossed a river when he left the city of Harran in modern day Turkey and crossed the Euphrates into Canaan. Both men

---

[4] "A Letter from Abdu-Heba of Jerusalem," EA 286 Amarna Tablets reshafim.org.
[5] Genesis 23:19

crossed over into the same area. This crossing over is why many Bible scholars believe Eber's name is the origin of the word Hebrew.

Abraham became *very* rich, and the people in Canaan noticed. Four hundred years later, his family had multiplied into millions of people. When they took over Canaan, the Canaanites and others were calling them habiru, a similar sounding name perhaps, but a different meaning.

As a side note there is another word archaeologists have found that is similar in meaning to habiru. It is *shasu*. It is from the Egyptian word to wander. *Shasu* is written in documents of the pharaohs hundreds of years after Abraham and perhaps a few dynasties after the Exodus.

But there is one point to make about the *shasu* here. One reference to the *shasu* is translated, "the land of the *shasu* of YHW." Here is a connection between a people and the YHWH God of the Bible. This inscription predates the Moabite Stone[6] making it the earliest extra biblical writing of Yahweh. Surprisingly, there is no debate that YHW means the God of the Bible.

Where is this land? A *shasu* inscription from Amarah in Sudan refers to *ra-ba-na* which is thought to be Labana, Syria mentioned in the Amarna Letters. If you'd like to know more, Michael Astour's research in *Festshrift Elmar Edel*, is one of the best sources for learning about the possible location(s) of the *shasu's* territory. Spoiler: All the locations of the YHW *shasu* were in or near ancient Canaan and Israel.

But were Hebrews, or even Eber, in Syria? It was part of ancient Canaan. Populated with Canaanites. Right?

The discovery of the Royal Archives in Ebla in 1974 upended many a theory. In his article "The Archives of Ebla and the Bible," Jeff A. Benner tells us Paolo Matthiae, the Professor of Archaeology at

---

[6] Also known as the Meshe Stele, the Moabite Stone is an inscription by King Mesha telling how he led Moab against King Omri of Israel and won, taking all of the YHWH articles from the Jews and giving them to his god, Chemosh. Dated to about 840 BC.

the University of Rome La Sapienza, had started a dig site in 1963 at Tel Mardikh, Syria, about thirty miles southwest of Aleppo. By 1968, after finding inscriptions mentioning Ebla, Matthiae suspected he had found the mysterious ancient city of Ebla described by other civilizations in their clay tablets.

In 1974 when 2,000 tablets, 4,000 fragments of tablets and 10,000 chips, in fact, the largest library known of its time was unearthed, Professor Matthiae's suspicions were confirmed.

The tablets revealed a language different from Akkadian, the only other language besides Sumerian scholars knew existed for the time period. They called this new language Eblaite. A few experts thought it looked a lot like Hebrew. After much debate, and confident claims to the contrary,[7] what was obvious to some finally had to be admitted: Eblaite was closely related to Hebrew, and it dated to the Third Millennium BC (3000-2001 BC).

Among the tablets and fragments were royal documents, dictionaries, encyclopedias, treatises, laws, agricultural and educational texts. Some of the texts were bilingual vocabulary lists written in Eblaite and Sumerian. Sumerian was a language scholars knew which helped linguists to translate the other tablets. The bilingual lists were among ancient school texts and were used for teaching foreign languages.

Another Italian archaeologist working at Tel Mardikh was also surprised by Ebla. Professor Giovanni Pettinato wrote in his article, "The Royal Archives of Tell Mardikh-Ebla," that texts in Ebla matched texts found in Sumer. But it was also revealed that Sumerian scribes had copied new knowledge from Ebla's texts. Thus, we witness one valuable reason for teaching languages, trading knowledge. This proved an exchange of information not thought possible in 2400 BC.

There were even religious texts. Dagon of Canaan was among oth-

---

[7] Thomas O'Toole, "Ebla Tablets: No Biblical Claims," *The Washington Post* Dec,9, 1979.

er gods listed in these ancient inscriptions. These finds supported an early use for the word Canaan and supported the Bible's identification of pagan gods in the region. What this seems to suggest is an eyewitness account of the biblical text.

Benner writes that peculiar spellings found in the Bible's original Hebrew and thought to be errors are actually older forms of Semitic words. (Semitic people and languages are related to Shem.) The pagan god Chemosh was correctly spelled *Kamāš* in the Bible. In Job 9:3, water was written *mw* which was the correct Semitic spelling in the Third Millennium BC instead of the modern *mey*. This is an important point and a valuable discovery.

There are more examples, but you probably realize the older forms of the words show the Bible's texts prove eyewitnesses and native speakers wrote the Old Testament. The writers used words common in their day but strange by the sixth century BC. Many state the book of Genesis was written during the years the Israelites were captives in Babylon around 586 BC. But the language of the Old Testament proves it was not. That the Old Testament was written in the sixth century BC is a constant erroneous claim by believers and unbelievers as we will see in our study of Abraham.

Benner gives us an example of one of Ebla's religious inscriptions: "Lord of heaven and earth: the earth was not, you created it, the light of the day was not, you created it, the morning light you had not yet made exist."[8]

Sounds a bit like the first chapter of Genesis doesn't it? Remember, Noah had passed all what he knew on to his children and grandchildren. His son Shem was still living, perhaps even near Ebla, during Abraham's lifetime. The creation account and Adam's history was not

---

[8] Jeff A. Benner, "The Archives of Ebla and the Bible," Ancient Hebrew Research Center.

lost literature. It was rejected, altered by many, but not lost.

Towns listed in the Bible were also found on the Ebla Tablets. And about personal names, there are thousands of first names inscribed in the Ebla Tablets, many identical to biblical names. We might stumble over reading what we think are odd names, but in the Third Millennium BC they were part of a top 100 Best Names for Your Baby list. Apparently Ishmael and Israel were popular names for boys. Even the name Abram is on the list in Eblaite as Ab-ra-mu.[9]

Dr. Clifford Wilson states, "Hebrew scholars recognize remarkable similarities to later Hebrew in the Old Testament, and Professor Pettinato himself states...'Many of these names occur in the same form in the Old Testament, so that a certain interdependence between the culture of Ebla and that of the Old Testament must be granted.' "[10] This implies Abraham lived very near to the time of Ebla.

But this connection between Ebla and the Bible annoyed modern Syrians. Remember, Ebla was located in a region that is today Syria. Modern Syrians have adopted Islam and are a mixed people of Arabic, Greek and Aramaic (Semitic) descent.

William E. Harris described what happened to Italian archaeologist Pettinato. Harris wrote:

> In 1976 Pettinato was refused access to photographs of newly discovered tablets in fear that he might find additional evidence that the Eblaites were the ancestors of Israel. According to David Freedman, it was when Pettinato discovered the word 'Israel' in the Eblaite tablets he got in hot water with the Syrians... Due to this pressure from Syria, Profes-

---
[9] Boyce Rensberger, "Ebla Ruins Shed Light on Early Urban Man," *New York Times,* Jan 16,1979.
[10] Clifford Wilson, "Ebla:Its Impact on Bible Records," Institute For Creation Research.

sors Pettinato and Matthiae publish very little that relates to the Bible.[11]

Did you catch that? Facts were suppressed because of politics. Who knows what information today has been discovered we may never have access to? Only a small portion of all discoveries have been published.[12]

Ancient Syria was thought to be a land of illiterate nobodies. It must have been disconcerting to many Syrians whose hopes rose at the Ebla discovery putting them on the intellectual map of ancient empires only to find that empire linked to their sworn enemy, the Israelites.

By 2018 all connections to the Bible had been methodically discredited by liberal scholars and evolutionists. But the truth is a little hard to ignore. So— we won't.

Ebla was an important commercial center consisting of about 140 acres with 260,000 people wanting to live in or near the city. It had rulers called *en* in Eblaite. They ruled for a set number of years like a term of office, but rulers could be re-elected.

There may have been one man who decided to change this.[13] His name was Ebrium, spelled Eb-uru-um or Eb-ur-um.[14] He turned the system into a kingship, *lugal* in Eblaite. It worked like a monarchy, passing from father to son. This man may have been the first total monarch to rule Ebla during the Second Kingdom around 2340 BC. Others think he was a vizier, a royal official.

According to Professor Pettinato, under King Ebrium the Ebla Empire reached its peak and even the Akkadian Empire had to pay

---

[11] William E. Harris, *From Man to God: An LDS Scientist Views Creation, Progression and Exaltation*, (Horizon Pub & Dist Inc Yakima, Washington), 52.

[12] Wiseman, D.J. & E. Yamauchi, *Archaeology And The Bible*. (London: Pickering & Inglis, 1980), 4-5.

[13] Ronald M. Glassman Springer, *The Origins of Democracy in Tribes, City-States and Nation-States*, Springer International Publishing, Google Books, 464-465.

[14] Giovanni Pettinato, "The Royal Archives of Tell Mardikh-Ebla," *The Biblical Archaeologist*, Vol. 39, No. 2 (May, 1976), pp. 44-52

Ebla taxes. Tablets record wars and commercial relations between Ebla, Mari, Aššur, Hattu and Akkad. The tablets may even give us a peek at the rising city of Carchemish, *Kār-kà-ni-iš*. They also name one of Aššur's rulers, Du-ud-jà, whom Pettinato thinks may have been Tudija, one of the tent dwelling kings of Assyria.

What is notable about this Eblaite king is his name. Ebrium is translated Eber in Hebrew. Remember Eber listed in Genesis 10 as one of Shem's descendants? We learned his name is considered by many to be the source of the word Hebrew. And he was related to Abraham. What is also notable about Genesis 10 is it is called the Table of Nations because the men named on the list are associated with regions that became countries and empires. So is this Eber of Ebla the biblical Eber?

Pettinato thought so, at least before he got kicked out of Syria. He noticed the addition of a new word for God when Ebrium was king. *Il* in Eblaite is the same as the Hebrew *El* for God and was already part of the Eblaite language. The word *Ya* became an Eblaite addition during Ebrium's kingship. Pettinato connected *Ya* to the later Hebrew YWH.

Another link to Eber is that he is related to Arphaxad, Peleg, Terah, Nahor, Haran and Serug— all names of towns mentioned in a geography tablet at Ebla. Scholar Michael C. Astour wrote that Ebla identified towns and filled in places on the map in northern Syria, southern Turkey, the Euphrates valley and the steppes around Ebla that were unknown to modern people.[15] Of course, the Bible had recorded those men's names and their towns long ago. They were listed as Abraham's ancestors. The names may suggest a relationship to the king of Ebla.

Some scholars agree with Pettinato that Eber of Genesis 10 is the

---

[15] Michael C. Astour, "Toponymy of Ebla and Ethnohistory of Northern Syria: A Preliminary Survey," *Journal of the American Oriental Society*, 108, no. 4 (1988), 550.

Eber of Ebla. The biblical Eber was about thirty-four when the language was divided at the Tower of Babel somewhere in Mesopotamia. He was Abraham's 5th great grandfather, and he lived 464 years. When Abraham was born, Eber was about 225 years old. Eber died when Abraham's grandson Jacob was 79. So, it is possible. Of course, when you live to be over 400 years old, anything is possible.

The important thing is the name Eber was found connected to a region the Bible indicated had Semitic connections with a man named Eber. But we don't know if our Eber was the king. So far the name found at Ebla only proves the name Eber existed and it was used as a name for a man.

While scholars have dated the Ebla library to around 2500 BC, the beginning of Ebla was earlier. Ebla controlled over sixty kingdoms and city-states at its height, including those of Sumer, but it was involved in many conflicts with them. It was destroyed three times and rebuilt twice. After its third defeat it existed as a village called Mardikh until the 7th century AD.

The dates here are given as scholars write them, but they are estimates and may not agree with the exact dates of the Bible. The dates serve to show us an order of events and, in the case of Abraham, prove the Bible revealed a time in history few knew existed.

The habiru are also mentioned in an Eblaite text about a conflict between the city of Ushu and the Assyrians. They were asked to help Uushu, but this was after Abraham and not connected to Joshua. At least we know habiru was a word Ebla used.

Another people identified with the habiru are the Amorites. The ancient city of Mari dates from 2800 BC-1760 BC. It came to an end when it was conquered by Babylon under Hammurabi. But from 2300 BC to its fall, it was the capital of the Amorites.

The Amorites were descended from Ham through his son Canaan and spoke a language similar to Hebrew. Amorite means mountaineer. Amorites are known as the Martu in *Enmerkar and the Lord of Aratta*. The Akkadians and Sumerians referred to them as Amurru.

Tell Harīrī or Mari lies west of the Euphrates River near Abu Kamal, Syria, approximately 200 miles southeast of Harran where Terah and Abraham lived for a while. It is also southeast of Ebla. Mari was a city built on purpose to take advantage of its location near trade routes in the Euphrates Valley.

An enterprising society, the people built canals connecting the city to the Euphrates River. Besides irrigation and water sources for the city, the canals were built for trading ships. One canal allowed ships to bypass a longer route on the river, leading it straight through but for a fee. Since Mari controlled the river, you can imagine the profit it made.

The region is a strategic military area even today. Abu Kamal, just north of Iraq, was involved in the Iraq War in 2008, controlled by ISIS in 2014, and was still involved in attacks in 2019.

The ancient city of Mari sat on a slope so that water from seasonal torrential rains would drain away from the dried, mudbrick dwellings— an important feature as you can imagine. Two walls circled the city. The outer wall protected it from occasional floods of the Euphrates, and the inner wall protected it from raiders. Its citizens even had indoor plumbing.

Ancient Mari had close bonds to the Sumerians and the city of Ur. Mari's kings are listed on the Sumerian King List. They built temples to Shamash the god Gilgamesh prayed to in the *Epic of Gilgamesh*. Another inscription mentioned the first king of Ur, Mesannepada. Some scholars think the Mari people traveled from Sumer to build Mari. Mari existed alongside Nuzi, Ebla, Egypt, Babylon and Assyria. It exchanged turtle and clam shells, lapis lazuli and gold with Ebla.

What is important to Christians about the Mari Archives is the relationship they reveal of the Mari citizens to the Hebrews. They shared common elements of culture and language like the people of Ebla.

In 1933 André Parrot, a French archaeologist, began an excavation at Mari that would last more than forty years. Over twenty thousand tablets were found, of which only a few thousand have been released to the public. There are several temples, palaces, many more inscriptions and seals. Like Ebla, it lists many names and places recorded in the Bible.

One tablet tells of a thousand captives taken from the towns of Harran and Nahūr. Nahor was Abraham's grandfather. It is not known through any archaeological texts if the town is connected to Abraham's grandfather, but the Bible reveals his family connection to the region. Abraham sent his servant to this area to get a wife for his son Isaac and called it his homeland. Many scholars are willing to connect Abraham's family to the towns named for them.

Both towns, Harran and Nahor, are mentioned in the Mari texts as making treaties with local kings against Mari. Mari was often putting down uprisings by those they called the habiru. Once, a Hurrian king took over Nahor. Urkesh was a nearby Hurrian town.

The Mari Texts talk of tribal migrations in the Euphrates area and Canaan much like Abraham's journey and those of his grandson Jacob. They also reveal cultural practices in common with the Old Testament. Among the customs are oldest sons receiving a double inheritance, a patriarchal and tribal social organization where the heads of families ruled like elders. Those elders could be nomadic shepherds who negotiated water rights with rulers of towns. Abraham and Isaac made agreements like that.

The tablets tell us donkeys were considered civilized for kings and horses were reserved for war, and that animals were slaughtered to make covenants between people. They even show that there were people who had become popular enough to rule called *šāpitum*, a judge. This is comparable to the Old Testament judges.

Like the Ebla tablets, the Mari tablets lists the names of gods worshipped by the people and the pagan rituals associated with them. They also show prophets of these gods giving divine messages to kings.

Later, the majority of the population of Mari became western Semites, specifically Amorites and their cousins the Suteans. Scholars believe the Amorites eventually became the largest population throughout Canaan. Wolfgang Heimpel tells us the Suteans paid a sheep tax to the Mari kings. Sometimes they helped the kings by guarding caravans but they usually attacked them.[16] They sound a lot like the habiru we learned about earlier, but these people are considered to be Amorites.

Abraham had friends who were Amorite and shared a common lifestyle with them. Our verse in Genesis 14 when Abraham was first called a Hebrew states "...for he was living among the Oaks of Mamre the Amorite." Some think he was called a Hebrew because of his connection with the Amorite brothers in this verse.

Some scholars think Abraham was an Amorite. They say his brother's name Haran means mountaineer, the same meaning as Amorite, which it does. Abraham lived in the same places, spoke a similar language and his lifestyle was similar to theirs.

The Bible, however, states Amorites were distant cousins of Abraham's, descended from Ham, Shem's brother. (Genesis 10:16) That said, and for the purpose of being fair, we know nothing of Abraham's mother. We do know the Bible says Abraham was not an Amorite. He was an Eberite, with family connections to the towns of northeast Syria in the land of the Mari and Ebla Empires.

---

[16] Wolfgang Heimpel, *Letters to the King of Mari: A New Translation, with Historical Introduction*, (Penn State University:Eisenbrauns, 2003) 26.

Some scholars link the Amorites with the habiru people who also helped kings and robbed caravans. Neither the Amorite nor the habiru seemed to have a good reputation. A Sumerian legend about a woman marrying a Martu, an Amorite, gives us a picture of what other cultures thought of them. In the story, the bride's friend is cautioning her about marrying such a person. Here is what she says:

> ...he is one who eats what Nanna forbids and does not show reverence. They never stop roaming about ......, they are an abomination to the gods' dwellings. Their ideas are confused; they cause only disturbance. He is clothed in sack-leather ......, lives in a tent, exposed to wind and rain, and cannot properly recite prayers. He lives in the mountains and ignores the places of gods, digs up truffles in the foothills, does not know how to bend the knee, and eats raw flesh. He has no house during his life, and when he dies he will not be carried to a burial-place. My girlfriend, why would you marry Martu?[17]

Nanna is a Sumerian god not someone's grandma, and truffles are a type of mushroom in this passage, not chocolate candy. Bending the knee is thought to be a reference to farming. The Bible describes one Amorite king, Og of Bashan, as a giant in Deuteronomy 3:11.

Even though the Amorites were at peace with Israel at times, God told the Israelites under Joshua to get rid of them. But the reason God gave didn't involve their appearance or table manners. Amorites were Ham's descendants through his son Canaan. Canaanites were made

---

[17] J.A. Black, G. Cunningham, Fluckiger-Hawker, E, Robson, E., and Zólyomi, G., *The Electronic Text Corpus of Sumerian Literature,* Oxford, 1998.

up of tribes who became increasingly rebellious against God. This included the Amorites. Hundreds of years after Abraham had Amorite neighbors, Joshua was told to wipe them out.

By all this research, we can confidently say Abraham may have shared in the common culture of the times along with the Amorites and habirus such as language, customs, and lifestyle, but he did not share their reputation or continued rebellion against God. He was not an Amorite. He was descended from Eber, and he really wanted to be a father, the exalted father like his father named him. But he knew that would take a miracle to achieve.

*A*bram stood in the predawn darkness; the trees still black silhouettes, a handful of stars still sparkling on the horizon. A guard dog barked in the distance; short deep rasps followed by a howl, echoed from the grassy slopes rising to the mountains. He turned toward the sound. But there were no answering barks from jackals. His flocks were out there with his shepherds, safe even though his men slept; the dogs watched.

He thought of the pillars. Yes. He squinted. There they were, their cold grey stone gleaming under the lightening sky. He imagined the leaves sculpted onto them and twining upwards, birds, snakes and insects, the same images tattooed on young children as charms.

He didn't need to imagine the statues there. Also carved from the grey stone, their eyes inlaid with jewels, their lips full but never speaking. Sin sometimes robed like a man, sometimes in the form of a bull, brought gifts to Enlil. And so had he. He knew the prayers chanted, whispered and sung to those gods. But they were not as strong or as dependable as the guard dogs.

He sighed. His father had been loyal to them. But Sin had never answered from his lofty heights. Not before Haran died, and not after. Abram searched the sky. The moon was nowhere to be found. And neither was Sin, he thought. The ancients had known about another God, One who knew them, protected them and could speak into a man's heart. Shem had kept the history. It was the story of hope he was searching for.

Suddenly a feeling rose from his belly. A burning. No, a fire, but not of heat. It pricked like flames, but it came from within, from his feet and *into his hands to his arms. He dropped to the ground.*

A bright, weightless light grew inside him or was it outside? He didn't know. It came with something else. A knowing. A sense of complete peace. A voice that spoke to him but not by sound.

The sun was breaking the horizon when he finally stood. A new day was descending on the town of 'Ûr. Women were rising to stir fires, weavers were readying fibers and merchants were dreaming of the day's possibilities.

Abraham wondered at the normalcy surrounding him. He laughed, a joyous realization sweeping over him. His life was about to change for the better, and all he had to do was follow instructions.

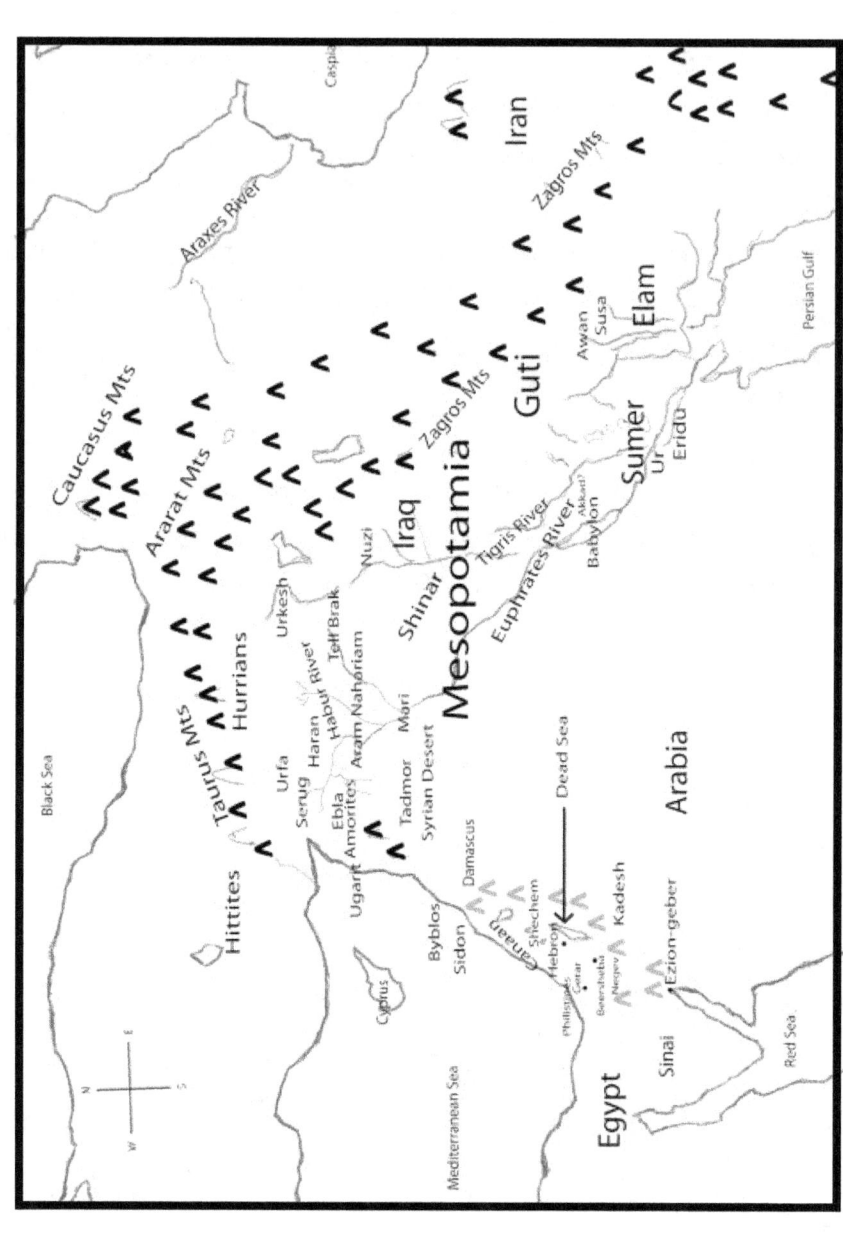

Chapter 2
Called Out From Ur

Along the Buranun River the ancient Sumerian civilization began. The Akkadians called the river Purattu. The Hebrews, Perath. The Elamites, Ufratush. The Greeks, the Euphrates.

If you had mentioned to Abraham that he grew up along the Euphrates River, he might have thought you stuttered. He did not call it by its Greek name. The Bible says Abraham lived in Ur. Ur was a major port city of the Persian Gulf, situated on the west bank near the mouth of the Euphrates in the Third Millennium BC. Today it is called Tell el-Muqayyar, Mound of Pitch.

Dove colored sand blankets the landscape in every direction during the dry season. Temperatures reach well over a hundred degrees. In this setting it might be hard to picture the marshes and sparkling blue waters of the ancient city. Aerial photos show a large walled area, first planned by King Ur-Nammu, but the city itself is much older, dating to the Ubaid people (3800 BC).

On this stretch of flat land, the people did not find much in natural resources besides water, reeds and mud. But what they did with these three things was remarkable.

Mud became their source for making tools like scythes to help harvest their grain. It became their writing pads to record events, government records, tax reports and school texts. It was used to make cups, bowls, jars and vases. It became bricks for building homes, temples, palaces and storage centers.

Reeds were woven into baskets, mats and even boats. Water was directed into irrigation channels. The rivers and the Gulf became a highway for trade.

These enterprising people influenced the entire world and still do today. Symbols for sounds, like in the English language, can be traced to wedge shapes pressed into clay, a writing method we call Sumerian cuneiform.

These people also studied astronomy and gave us number systems based on one, ten and six. The system based on six, in which numbers used are divisible by six, is the base for how to tell time. So when you look at a clock, or consider that a day is twenty-four hours, a month is thirty days, twelve months are in a year, historians say you can thank the Sumerians. But much of this knowledge was probably brought into the world after the flood by Noah and his family.

At Ur, ancient royal tombs, organized neighborhoods, musical instruments, literature, poems, schools and libraries revealed a rich culture. Ur was a merchant city with the latest news, goods and designs of Mesopotamia pouring into and out of its boundaries. Farmers brought in livestock and crops for rituals and sacrifices, for wool, hides and food. Gold came from as far away as Aratta (Armenia), Turkey, Iran and Dilmun. Wood came from Canaan or India.

Two major trade routes followed the Tigris and Euphrates north and along their tributaries. Another branched off at Mari into the Syrian Desert toward the oasis of Tadmor (Palmyra).

Ur's merchants traded with people from the Indus civilization over a thousand miles away for rust colored gems called carnelian. These gems were carved into beads. The merchants traveled to modern day Afghanistan to get the rich blue lapis lazuli rock and polished stones which were used to make jewelry, idols, government seals and other decorations. Copper came from Oman. Chlorite, a mineral, came from Iran and was used by craftsmen to carve seals, beads and to form goblets and containers ranging in color from dark green to light gray. Some vessels were dedicated to Sumerian gods.

These gemstones and minerals are found at archaeological excavations all over Mesopotamia and the farthest reaches of the time. What we know then is that people traveled and traveling far was not uncommon. We also know they could read, write and do math as the merchant records engraved on clay tablets tell us. They could plan, build and share information, obvious by the city, its schools, libraries and shared culture of the surrounding regions.

People wanted to live near Ur because a poor person could be educated and become rich or at least better off. Houses were unearthed that had stairs leading to the roof and had rooms built off a central courtyard. They resemble the modern homes of families in Iraq today.

Towering over the city was the ziggurat built by Ur-Nammu for Nanna, the moon god. Nanna was also called Su'en or Sin. Archaeologists think he may be shown sitting on a throne on the Ur-Nammu Stele. But his most common image is that of a bull or a crescent. Golden bulls were found on lyres (The Great Lyre) and charms. Others think the bull is Shamash, god of the sun, like in the *Epic of Gilgamesh.*

Abraham is thought to have lived in this rich, ancient city. He is known as the father of the Israelites. But Abraham did not start out in Israel. Many think he was born in Ur, Iraq.

Or was he?

The location of Abraham's Ur has been debated. There was more than one Ur in Mesopotamia. The city we just described held great influence over all Mesopotamia— or was it the other way around? Archaeologists see a north to south migration first in the Halaf and Ubaid cultures. Following this period is another migration, the Uruk Expansion, originating from this southern area and going out in all directions. Cities with Ur as part of their names ranged from the south of Iraq to Turkey.

Ur in Hebrew means to give light or shine. The word was probably connected to the chief god of the city, Nanna/Sin, whether sun or moon. Abraham's Ur is thought to be either in southern Iraq, the great Ur of the ancient world, or it is one of two Urs in northern Mesopotamia. The truth is the Bible never says Abraham was born in Ur. It says he was living there.

Christians may be tempted to connect Abraham to the Ur in Iraq because it was part of the Sumerian civilization and known for its highly civilized culture. A man as important as Abraham surely lived in such a place. Right? But Mesopotamia was a land of civilized cultures located in the south, north, east and west during Abraham's lifetime. Archaeology has proved this as we learned in the last chapter.

Someday someone may decipher a tablet or stumble upon a grand discovery that will settle the debate. For now let's take a look at the Urs scholars connect to Abraham because we can find out more about the world he lived in. Then, you can pick your favorite Ur.

Northern Mesopotamia: Urkesh and Urfa

Northern Mesopotamia has two locations in the Khabur River area, Urkesh and Urfa, that are good alternative candidates for Abraham's Ur. At least one reason for this conclusion is because it seems ridiculous Terah and Abraham would travel north from the Ur in southern Iraq to Harran in Turkey, and then cross the Euphrates into Canaan.[1] It would have been more sensible to cross at Mari, since the long way was a thousand mile trip.

But travel plans aside, these northern Urs are in a prime spot concerning biblical ties to Abraham. There are at least two cities with Ur as part of their name near Harran. Harran itself is in a location where settlement is traditionally dated to 9000 BC. Göbekli Tepe is in this region, one of the oldest known sites in the world. Remember, traditional dating may not agree with the Bible, but what this tells us is Göbekli Tepe was among the first settlements after the flood in an area near Mt. Ararat.

Which makes one wonder: if the oldest sites are found in the north, did civilization spread from Sumer or to it?

Some archaeologists are declaring, to it; the regions of the northern Middle East are where civilization began.[2] In the same period are uncommonly large settlements in the Amuq Plain. Curiously, these larger groups separated into smaller ones for a time and moved. This area in Turkey and northeast Syria is a goldmine for archaeologists. There are over 200 sites, and discoveries are yet to be made at places like Tell Kurdu and Tayinat.

Our first northern Ur is Urkesh, modern Tell Mozan in northeast Syria, about 400 miles from Damascus. It was a Hurrian city that existed at the same time as Ebla and Mari. The Hurrians spoke a language unrelated to Hebrew, Sumerian or Indo-European. Discoveries at the site since its excavation in 1984 show Hurrian culture reaches back

---
[1] Cyrus H. Gordon, "Where Is Abraham's Ur?" *Archaeology Review* 3:2 June 1977.
[2] Trustees of the British Museum, "Domuztepe Excavation of a Late Neolithic settlement in south-central Turkey," The British Museum.

to 3000-2500 BC. The 300 acre city was bigger than Ebla.[3] Located almost a hundred miles slightly north and east of Harran, it was an important trade city lying on the east west route.

Tell Brak is nearby and is a site considered by some to be a possible location for the lost city of Akkad and near the location for the real Tower of Babel.[4] Chagar Bazar is also in the vicinity and shows evidence of the Halaf and Ubaid cultures prior to the Tower of Babel account.

Historians believed Urkesh to be founded after the Akkadian Empire fell. But archaeologists and husband and wife team, Georgio Buccellati and Marilyn Kelly-Buccellati have discovered the real history of Urkesh is older than anyone thought. They have also found the Hurrians were more advanced than first believed, having plumbing and architecture to rival other sites in Mesopotamia. What this means is this city was as advanced and important in trade as the Ur in southern Iraq.

Nuzi was another Hurrian city and excavations there (Yorghan Tepe) have given us the Nuzi Tablets. These inscriptions support the traditions written by the patriarchs concerning slaves inheriting property (Genesis 15:2), possessing household gods as proof of a legal right to an estate (Genesis 31:19), children through a concubine (Genesis 16:2-3), blessings pronounced over children from dying parents (Genesis 27:4), selling a birthright (Genesis 25:29-34) and family records being kept.

There are some scholars who argue the Nuzi Tablets have nothing to do with the patriarchs, but the evidence points to the contrary. Nuzi was an ancient city connected to other ancient cities—like Urkesh— during the time of the patriarchs, recording the life of the ancient

---

[3] Giorgio Buccellati and Marilyn Kelly-Buccellati, "In Search of Hurrian Urkesh City of Myth," *Odyssey*, May/June 2001, pg 24.

[4] Anne Habermehl, "Where in the World Is the Tower of Babel?" *Answers Research Journal*, Vol.4, March 23, 2011, p. 25-53.

world's ordinary, average citizen in legal documents. It dealt with the Hurrian culture which Harry Hoffner, Professor in the Oriental Institute and a leading Hittite scholar, says were the Hivites and perhaps the Jebusites of the Bible.[5] The Hivites and Jebusites were Canaanites, people descended from Canaan, the son of Ham.

What archaeology has shown is the widespread culture of Mesopotamia had many common elements with Abraham's Hebrew life as described in Genesis. Abraham was not isolated from social practices in the north or south. He was separated by his religious beliefs, however, as we will see.

Remember the cities of Abraham's ancestors, Serug and Nahor? They were in the same region as Urkesh. Historian Patricia Berlyn states Sarai and Milcah are similar names of Hurrian goddesses, Sarnatum and Malkatu. Urkesh was eventually conquered by the Hittites and Assyrians.

The second northern Ur lies directly west of Urkesh. The Ebla Tablets mention a city called Urfa near Harran. Some scholars believe this Ur to be Abraham's hometown.

Göbekli Tepe is six miles northeast of Urfa. It had a huge religious center dedicated to pagan gods. Even though this site may have been abandoned by Abraham's day, it is important to remember Abraham's father, Terah, worshipped idols. Joshua 24:2 says, "And Joshua said unto all the people, Thus saith the LORD God of Israel, Your fathers dwelt on the other side of the flood in old time, even Terah, the father of Abraham, and the father of Nachor: and they served other gods."

Joshua may be indicating this region had a reputation for idols. Harran, like Ur, was a major center of worship for Sin, the Moon God.

---

5 William Harms, "Evidence of battle at Hamoukar points to early urban development," *The University of Chicago Chronicle* Vol. 26 No.8 Jan. 18, 2007.

We learned in Chapter 1 the city of Mari, was about 200 miles south of Harran in northern Syria. The Mari and Ebla texts, like the Nuzi Tablets, revealed a world exactly as the Bible described it in the Old Testament era of Abraham and his sons and grandsons. The Mari and Ebla texts also included Hebrew names, Abram, Noah, Jacob, Ishmael, Dan, the tribes of Levi and Benjamin, etc., and many Hebrew words. These northern cities, Urkesh and Urfa included, dated to the time of Abraham and were connected by trade and politics.

Also in the first chapter we learned that besides mentioning Harran, the Ebla and Mari texts mentioned the cities of Nahor and Serug. The Bible says Nahor was Abraham's grandfather. Serug was his great grandfather. The town called Serug is thought to be Suruç today, about thirty miles southwest of Urfa. Weaving was an important trade there.

Urfa was a trading center, and later conquered by all the major empires, including Sumer, Ebla, Babylon and Akkad. In other words, it shared common elements of their cultures. Islamic tradition favors this area as well as some Jewish scholars. Urfa is called Sanliurfa today. Clustered around it are ancient temples and settlements and Turkey's largest museum complex.

In 2015, this area was involved in the war against ISIS and Sanliurfa and Suruc became refugee cities for the Kurdish people.

The northern Urs also have a strong Biblical connection according to Abraham's own testimony. Verses like Genesis 25:20 and Deuteronomy 26:5 say Abraham's family was Syrian, *ărammîy* which is Aramaic. His nephew Laban spoke Aramaic in Genesis 31:47. Abraham told his servant his homeland was where his brother lived in *Ăram Nahărayim*, Aram of the two rivers. (Genesis 24:4-10) This is translated Mesopotamia in many Bibles, but it indicates a northern location.

The Bible scholars who favor the northern locations do so on the biblical evidence Urkesh and Urfa provide and the idea that a longer trip from southern Iraq to Turkey was not common sense. The city of Urfa has been chosen as the most likely Ur by some experts, Urkesh by others.

Southern Mesopotamia: Ur, Iraq

Interest in southern Iraq began to build as Sir Austen Henry Layard began excavating ancient Babylonian cities there. Layard, born in France but working for England, loved to travel. In 1840, he became interested in a ruin thought to be built by Nimrod. A friend, French archaeologist Paul Émille Botta, was digging at a site known as Khorsabad, and his discoveries encouraged Layard to investigate his ruin.

Galloping across steppes on horses, keeping secrets from dangerous sultans and warring tribes, pacifying locals who thought his finds were idols, trying to prevent valuable reliefs from crumbling when exposed to air, befriending the Christians of Mosul, Layard recorded his adventures in a book called, *Ninevah And Its Remains.*[6] It is an interesting read.

Back in England, those who were reluctant to support Layard's efforts changed their minds when he sent back winged bulls and other treasures from the Assyrian Empire. But soon the money for his expedition ran out, and Layard left Iraq.

In the meantime, a man named Henry Rawlinson was learning to read the scratchings on tablets called cuneiform. In 1849, he read an inscription on a brick brought back to England by another archaeologist. His translation surprised everyone. The brick said Ur.

Desiring more treasure, the British contacted their consul in Basra, Iraq to see if he could find any. He did. He started whacking away at a ziggurat and uncovered two cylinders. The British Museum was disappointed until the cylinders were deciphered. They identified Nabonidus and his son Belshazzar from the book of Daniel.

---

[6] Read it online here: https://archive.org/details/ninevehanditsre03layagoog

But the site was abandoned because the treasures from ancient Assyria were better, and it wasn't until the 1920s that C. Leonard Woolley started work near the large ziggurat. Who knows what was looted or destroyed in the sixty years the site lay deserted? Woolley eventually rediscovered Ur, *Urim*, and announced this was Abraham's Ur.

Ur dates to the Ubaid period, roughly 6500-3800 BC, so it too is an ancient city. The Ubaid period comes before the Uruk Expansion which Bible scholars say is really the dispersal of people after the Tower of Babel.[7] The Uruk movement originated from the area around Eridu.

Woolley was good at creating publicity, but some of his conclusions have proven false. For instance, he thought the Royal Tombs were full of loyal servants who willingly drank poison to follow their king into the afterlife. Examinations of the skeletons in 2009 showed these people were violently executed in a ritual of human sacrifice.[8] The following funeral preparations were also gruesome.

Agatha Christie, a famous British author, was married to Woolley's assistant Max Mallowan. She said, "Leonard Woolley saw with the eye of imagination: the place was as real to him as it had been in 1500 B.C., or a few thousand years earlier. Wherever he happened to be, he could make it come alive. While he was speaking I felt in my mind no doubt whatever that the house on the corner had been Abraham's. It was his reconstruction of the past and he believed in it, and anyone who listened to him believed in it also."[9]

But announcing it as Abraham's Ur and imagining it as such did not mean that it was. Many respected scholars agreed with him, how-

---

[7] You can read more about the Tower of Babel in *NOAH* by Flying Eagle Publications.

[8] John Noble Wilford, "At Ur, Ritual Deaths That Were Anything but Serene," *The New York Times*, October 26, 2009.

[9] Richard L. Zettler, "Treasures From The Royal Tombs Of Ur," Ur of the Chaldees, The Oriental Institute University of Chicago, 1998.

ever, that this site was the biblical Ur. The majority of modern scholars are willing to agree with him too. But does the Bible?

The Biblical *Ûr*

The Bible states Abraham's father lived in *'ûr* of the *kaśdîy,* Ur of the Chaldees. It uses the phrase Ur of the Chaldees every time, four times, that it mentions Ur. It seems to be important and used like a finger pointing to an exact location. But where?

Although there is more than one city containing the sound for Ur, experts return to the sites we've already discussed as the most likely. To choose the right Ur, we need to know which one is of the Chaldees. Unfortunately that is not as easy as it sounds. There may be evidence pointing to a northern location and a southern one. Following the experts' research is a bit like riding a merry-go-round. Here we go...

Bible scholar Cyrus H. Gordon says, "...Sumerian Ur is never called 'Ur of the Chaldees' in any of the numerous references to Ur in the cuneiform tablets."[10] Chaldeans are known to have lived in southern Iraq, however. The problem is the first mention of Chaldea was by Ashurbanipal, an Assyrian king who lived around 884 BC, much later than Abraham or even Moses who wrote Genesis.

To many experts this problem proves Moses did not write Genesis. They insist it was written much later while the Israelites were captives in Babylon. But the Ebla Tablets have proven otherwise.

Who then was the writer who indicated Chaldea? Is there any evidence to solve the puzzle? The solution may be in understanding the word translated as Chaldees.

According to *Strong's*, the word translated Chaldees is *Kasdîy* (kass DEEN). It refers to an astrologer or a descendant of Kesed, a Kasdite. Kesed

---

[10] Cyrus H. Gordon, "Where Is Abraham's Ur?" *Biblical Archaeology Review* 3:2, June 1977.

is listed as one of Nahor's sons in Genesis 22:22. He is Abraham's nephew.

Kasdîy can even mean toward the Kasdites. The *Jewish Encyclopedia* tells us that the Hebrew is the oldest construction of the word. The Babylonian and Assyrian forms are later renderings sometimes spelled *Kalde*. That is a valuable clue, and may be a similar instance of what we learned in Chapter 1 about Hebrew words discovered on the Ebla Tablets being in their original form.

An ancient Greek soldier mentioned Chaldeans fighting with Arameans near the Black Sea.[11] That is farther north than Urfa. All this seems to indicate a northern location for a biblical "Chaldee."

Kasdîy may have indicated astrologers. Unfortunately astrologers were everywhere in Mesopotamia, even in Mari and farther north. But according to historians, Sumerians were the first astrologers after the flood. This may be wrong, however, if you consider the discoveries at Göbekli Tepe and its surrounding sites. Astrology may have been brought to Iraq.

Scholars state this kind of worship began in Iraq before Sumer at Eridu. Later, the Babylonians were also famed astrologers. Moses would have known about either group because it is thought the Middle Kingdom of Babylon dates to 1595 BC, over a hundred years before the Exodus.

Scholars who favor a southern Ur state the word Chaldees was added by a scribe to make it clear to later readers which Ur was Abraham's— the southern location. This reasoning does have a foundation in the Bible.[12]

At any rate, the Ur in southern Iraq was controlled by astrologers, Sumerian and Babylonian, for a long time. It was the city of a great pagan temple and this may be what distinguished this Ur from any

---

[11] Ashley Cooper, *The Whole Works of Xenophon* (London: Jones & Co 1832) 44.
[12] "City of Rameses" in Exodus1:11 and 12:37 was added by a scribe so later readers would know where the Israelite slaves lived since it was built over their town, Avaris.

similarly named city somewhere else. But, we must remember this type of religion spread throughout Mesopotamia after the Tower of Babel.

Just for fun, you might like to know the Chaldeans (884 BC) from the south, who began the New Babylonian Empire after Moses' time, were also famous astrologers and may have had a connection to the Hebrews too. Their first king was Sumu-abi which scholars think could mean Shem is my father. Or, maybe you didn't really need to know that...

There is one more important theory we need to cover about the word *Kasdîy*. Some scholars wonder if it has any connection to the Kassites who conquered the Babylonians and were the rulers during the Middle Kingdom of the Babylonian Empire, the one a hundred years before Moses. Kassites were from the Zagros Mountains which curve around the Fertile Crescent to the west of the Tigris and stretch north to the Turkey Syria border.

The early Kassites may also have ties to the Guti, an Akkadian word for Kardu (Also spelled Qartu or Qarti). The Kardu are mentioned in Sumerian tablets. Ancient Kardu territory includes Halah and Habor mentioned in 2Kings 17:6 and called the cities of the Medes.[13] The Guti conquered the Akkadians and ruled Mesopotamia for a hundred years. But this period was a dark age because they were poor rulers.

So we've gone full circle, putting the Chaldeans in the north, then in the south, and...back in the north. It is time to get off the merry-go-round and digest what we've learned.

We have discovered a northern or a southern location for Ur doesn't really matter if you want Abraham to be civilized. Ur was a rich and cultured city in its day. But Urkesh and Urfa were linked to other developed, thriving cities with a shared culture between them and the southern Ur. It is not far-fetched to think Abraham could have learned to read, write

---

[13] Modern Kurds are thought to be descended from the Kardu.

or do math in either location. According to archaeological texts, Abraham was an average guy living near the average town. It was only when he obeyed God's invitation his life became anything but ordinary.

And, all the Chaldeans may be related to the Hebrews? Obviously there is something we are misunderstanding here. (For the record, we are putting our money on Kesed, the nephew and his clan.)

We've also learned trade routes ran from southern Ur up to Harran and trading caravans traveled long distances, even to the Black Sea and beyond.[14] The route from Ur, Iraq to Harran is not an impossible theory then. Also, consulting the map, the shortcut from Mari into Canaan along the Palmyra route would have meant crossing a harsh desert plain with livestock. If Abraham was traveling from Iraq, it may be why he went north around the desert.

More important, while either a northern or southern Ur is a possible choice for where Abraham was living, there is no archaeological evidence and no clear biblical link to southern Iraq as his birthplace. Abraham himself points north to a homeland in Genesis 24.

The Bible is crystal clear in the word *Ăram Năhărayim* the part of Mesopotamia it is pointing out is the northern reaches of the Tigris and Euphrates Rivers. Also, there is evidence, secular and biblical, that points north[15] for the homeland of ancient Chaldeans before they took over Empires.

It is evident from the Genesis account that Abraham said his family and his country were in the area of modern Syria and Turkey. It says he was living there and he left there. His brother was born in Ur, and he died there. "And Haran died before his father Terah in the land of his nativity, in *'Ûr* of the Chaldee [*Kasdîy*]." (Genesis 11:28)

---

[14] Alan R. Millard, "Where Was Abraham's Ur?" *Biblical Archaeology Review* 27:3, May/June 2001.

[15] Thomas Gale, "Chaldea, Chaldeans," Encyclopaedia Judaica, Encyclopedia.com, 2007.

Notice that God told Abraham to get out of his country, where he was living, Ur, and then told him to leave his family who were in Syria/Turkey. The only family leaving Ur with Abraham besides his wife was his dad and his nephew. His brother, Nahor, to whom he later sent his servant, may have already been living near the borderlands of Syria and Turkey. Nahor may have always lived there. The important aspect of the story was God was making it plain to Abraham, "Go. I am giving *you* a new land."

And that's the story of the two, um, three Urs.

Abraham must have been amazed by the presence of the true God of the universe. Surrounded by false gods like gold bulls, elaborately engraved statues of man-like gods, his family immersed in their worship of them, Abraham may have started life worshipping them too. But something happened in his heart to show him they were only gods of stone and wood, gods with fake jeweled eyes and mouths that could not speak.

He probably saw the clay masks of Humbaba, the guardian of the Cedar Forests. He knew by heart the images of Nanna and Scorpion Man in the temples. He heard the music from the lyres with their golden bulls for heads. He may have even heard the lyres play music for his brother Haran's funeral. But one day, the Creator of Heaven and Earth spoke to him and said, "Leave this behind you."

Cities were safer than the open country. They were walled and had armies. Nomads were settled outside the walls. They roamed far into the wild and were seen near trade routes. Abraham may have thought about the dangers of leaving '*Ûr*. His father was old, his nephew young. But this God who spoke to him he could not ignore. His presence was genuine, compelling.

How old was Abraham when God first appeared to him in '*Ûr* of the *Kasdîy*? Abraham does not say. But his story must have convinced

Terah. Some scholars state Abraham was seventy when God first spoke to him. They begin to count the travels of the children of Israel and the giving of the law as stated in Exodus 12:40-41 and Galatians 3:17 from Abraham's call. To say Abraham received his call when he was seventy fits with what we know of his character. He obeyed immediately.

But Genesis 11:31 says it was Terah's decision to go to Canaan. Some think Terah was inspired to move because of the tragic death of his son Haran. The word translated before, "And Haran died before his father Terah," means in the presence of or on the face. These scholars interpret a tragedy of some kind had happened to Haran.

Other changes came to this family. Genesis 11:29 says, "And Abram and Nahor took them wives: the name of Abram's wife was Sarai; and the name of Nahor's wife, Milcah, the daughter of Haran, the father of Milcah, and the father of Iscah."

Terah wrote his portion of the family record and signed it in Genesis 11:27. There used to be a show on television called *My Three Sons*. You may not have heard of it because it was filmed before there were color tvs. It was about a man who was a widower and was raising his three sons. The Bible has a pattern about a man and his three sons.

Adam had three sons listed in Genesis. Of course he had more, but we are focusing on these three: Cain Abel and Seth. God chose Seth to continue the family line to Noah. Noah also had three sons: Ham Shem and Japheth. They are listed from the youngest to the oldest. We have to read other verses to find that out because Noah only tells us how old he was when his first son was born.

Terah listed his sons the same way. Terah says he was seventy when he had Abram, Nahor and Haran. This doesn't mean they were triplets. Terah was seventy when he had Haran. He was 205 when he died, and Abram was seventy-five when he left Harran to go to Canaan.

If we do the math, 205 minus 75, and assume Abraham left Harran the same year his father died, then Terah was 130 when Abraham was born. And Terah's oldest son, Haran, was sixty when Abraham was born. Can you imagine having an older brother who is sixty years older? Today that is old enough to be your grandpa!

Well, then you can see how Haran would have daughters old enough to marry his brothers. But here is something you may not have thought about. Why didn't Lot inherit Haran's property? He was Haran's son. Instead, Terah takes him to live with him. It may mean there was no property. They could have lost it in a local skirmish over territory or a greater battle between cities. The era of the Uruk Expansion was not always peaceful.

And what about Haran's wife? If Haran's wife were living, she, as a widow, would have been in charge of the property until the children were adults. Because she had children, she had choices. She could have returned to her family or, if she had a source of income, she could have remained in her home. Lot, who must have been unmarried, would have received a share so that he would be able to purchase a bride in the future. But nothing is said about any of this.

Haran's daughter Milcah was given to Nahor as a wife which would be very wrong today, but those laws came later. Nahor would have received a portion of Haran's property or money as her inheritance if there was any. It was hers legally and would have returned to her if Nahor had died or divorced her.

We don't know what happened to Haran's other daughter Iscah. Jewish tradition says Iscah was another name for Sarai, but we cannot prove that. (We will talk about Sarai in another chapter.)

Terah as the father of the family had an obligation to see his family provided for and protected. If Abraham had told him about God visiting him and the message God gave him, Terah might have taken it upon himself to go with him. Perhaps he was in failing health and Abraham was taking care of him. Nahor seems to have been busy with his own household.

For whatever reason, Terah decided to move to Canaan. Terah was well over 130 years old. According to some scholars he was 200 years old. He made it to the city of Harran and stopped. If he was coming up from Ur, Iraq, we are not surprised. They needed to regroup for the next hike south. The regroup lasted years if that is what happened.

But if he came from the north, why stop? The area may have been embroiled in one of the many skirmishes and battles of the day and Harran was safe. Perhaps the grand temple of Sin caught his eye. Some scholars think Terah was a traveling merchant. Harran was in a good spot for trading. But maybe he was too old to travel any farther.

The Bible says they settled there. The word is *yâshab,* to sit down. Abraham's brother Nahor built his small empire in the area. Abraham prospered there too. But what about Canaan? Did Abraham give up on the word God had spoken to him?

*T*he band traveling with them veered off on the west road toward the great waters. Large cities awaited them there. The surrounding plain, heavy with its fields of grain, embraced them. He wondered if the coastal cities would.

Abram turned away. He was surprised Sarai stood watching too. He hadn't heard her come up behind him.

"Father needs to rest again," she said. "I can wait with a party of servants. Lot will remain. You can go on into the city if you wish."

"No," Abram replied. "You and I stay together." He nodded to the south. "I will send Yitro ahead to arrange matters for us."

She said nothing, but her eyes, colored like honey, seemed troubled.

He put his arm around her small, narrow shoulders. He glanced again at the families and traders in the distance, their ox carts peeling a layer of dust from the road that curled upward after them. El, he thought. El surely led them as the ox guided the wagons.

He pointed to them. "What is El, Sarai?"

She frowned. "The God?"

"The word."

"A staff." She thought a moment. "The Strong Authority. The Ox in the Yoke."

"Yes." He smiled. "We walk alongside like the second ox. And like a shepherd He is leading us and will protect us."

She stared at the ground, the wind blowing her scarf against her cheek and hiding her expression from him. But he knew her thoughts. Fear.

"The habiru...They are here, Abram." She looked behind them toward the city gates of Harran. "Here," she whispered. She closed her eyes and a tear ran down her cheek.

Abram softened at the sight of her as he always did. He knew the vi-

sions of terror playing in the black shadows behind her trembling eyelids. The screams of war echoed even in his ears. The rush of advancing men and thundering feet. The fear. Always the fear. "But we are habiru," *he told her.* "They call us habiru."

Drawing herself up, she nodded. She was a good woman, he thought. Even though she was small and thin with the appearance of youth about her. If only... But he pushed those thoughts away— again.

"I must tend to Father," *she said.*

He caught her hand as she turned from him. "El, the Might One is yoked with us. He is our help. Trust Him, Sarai, please."

Her cheeks, high and round, were flushed from the sun. "I am trying," *she said.*

Abram let go of her hand. The city gates shone white in the hot afternoon light. He could see them even from this distance. Inside them people clustered in homes, mud huts strengthened with the straw from harvested grain and lined up like fruit in the traders rack. The people received their rations of grain, worshipped their silent gods and looked upon him sometimes with dread, sometimes with curiosity.

He had never been to Harran much less stepped foot past its gates. But he knew it. Harran was the same as every other city. He surveyed the plain. There. Water from a river sparkled in the distance. A place set apart. Free. He would tell Yitro he wanted that parcel for their camp.

He walked back to Terah, resting in the shade of a makeshift shelter. His face was pale and he was breathing heavily again. Abram appealed to the Voice who had spoken into his heart, but there was no answer. Terah gave him a feeble smile, and Abram sat down on a rock next to him.

He wanted to smile back. But El's silence shook him. A vague feeling rose inside, and it came with a thought. Was El really with him?

Chapter 3
Canaan

Abraham arrived in Harran sometime after his brother's death. Harran was situated on a flat plain, northeast of the Euphrates near the Balikh River. An archaeological site at Tell Sabi Abyad has shown that pottery was produced there for the trade market. Clay tokens, used for exchange, date to 5,000 BC by an evolutionary timeline. Cattle, pigs, sheep and goats were raised along with einkorn wheat, barley, flax, lentils and peas.

The area continued to be inhabited throughout the time of the major empires. Its location near the Balikh gave it its importance. Harran lay about six hundred miles north, by river, from Ur, Iraq. Like a shimmering, liquid ribbon, the Euphrates connected the trade cities and both were major centers of worship for Sin.

When God first spoke to Abraham, Abraham may not have known Him. God's voice in Abraham's heart may have been unfamiliar. So when he arrived with his father in a thriving religious city, we cannot assume Abraham fully understood the message God had given him. We learned in the last chapter that the Bible said they settled, *yâshab,* they sat down. Terah seems to be the one who made the decision.

Abraham's homeland, Aram Naharaim, stretched south of Harran, along the Balikh and Euphrates Rivers. So, it doesn't seem they got very far. Why?

Some Bible scholars say Abraham continued his trip to Canaan after dropping his father off in Harran; then Terah died sixty years later. Theses scholars think Abraham was Terah's oldest son. But this theory ignores Acts 7:2-4 which says Abraham left Harran after Terah died.

The other scholars who say Abraham was seventy when God called him think Terah was the reason for the stop in Harran. Many believe Abraham had to delay his move to Canaan because of his father's health.

The biblical chronology is:
- God spoke to Abraham in Ur
- Terah and Abraham moved
- Terah died
- God spoke to Abraham again
- Abraham left Harran

The Bible does not say how long Abraham lived in Harran. It depends on when scholars begin calculating the 400-430 years of Israel's bondage, but many think Abraham spent five years in Harran. There is also no evidence that God spoke to Abraham during the time between moving to Harran and Terah's death.

There was another instance when God was silent in Abraham's life. It was when Abraham took Sarah's advice and had a son named Ishmael. It was a big mistake and a delay. This could have been the situation in Harran. Abraham may have listened to Terah and stayed in Harran. Or, Terah whom Abraham brought along got sick, and Abraham had to wait in Harran.

Which points to the fact that Abraham was not supposed to have Terah with him in the first place. God's words to Abraham were to leave his family and his father's house. But, he packed everybody up to move. Terah and Lot among the stuff.

God was not mad at Abraham...yet. He is patient with us on our journey of learning to trust Him. Abraham was acting according to his society and respecting the ruler of the family, the patriarch. It was what he knew to do. It was not what God told him to do.

Some scholars think there were other reasons for Terah's desire to move to Canaan since we cannot be sure if Abraham told his father God appeared to him. We assume he would tell Terah because it was an amazing thing to happen. It was also Abraham's habit to obey immediately. But to be thorough, let's take a look at these scholars' ideas and their dates for Abraham to see what we find out.

Abraham is commonly dated on an evolutionary timeline to the Third Dynasty of Ur and later, either 2112-2004 BC or anywhere from 2017-1763 BC. Some scholars date him during the Dynasty of Gutium, 2217- 2120 BC. In Chapter 2 we said the Gutium Dynasty was a period of dark ages in Mesopotamia. Some think this state of decline was the reason Terah wanted to move out of the area of Sumer.

But other scholars hold up the Ebla Tablets and say the kings and pharaohs they mention and fail to mention place Abraham in the Early Dynastic period, about 2500 BC on a traditional timeline. Matt McClellen, David Down and others date Abraham to the Early Bronze Age I using the Bible and archaeology as their guide. Dr. A. J. M. Osgood said that the Bible account places Abraham going into Canaan in 1875 BC when he was seventy-five.[1] This means Abraham was born in 1950 BC. But he thinks Abraham's world as described in the Bible dates to the Jemdat Nasr period or pre Early Dynastic I.

---

[1] Dr. A.J.M. Osgood *The Times of Abraham* Journal of Creation 2(1):77–87, April 1986 Creation.com.

Dr. Osgood is showing us it is the Bible that dates what is called the Early Bronze Age 1, Early Dynastic and Jemdat Nasr periods to around 1950 BC and before. After the flood in roughly 2348 BC, about 400 years passed and Abraham was born. During this 400 years we must fit the Halaf and Ubaid people, events like the Tower of Babel, the migration of people (Uruk Expansion) and the building of cities. If you think this is not enough time, you might like to investigate the LXX version of the Bible.[2]

The 400 years is a rounded number. According to the Masoretic Text, Abraham was born 352 years after the flood. Noah died two years before Abraham was born. Shem, Arphaxad, Salah, Eber, Reu and Serug were still living when Abraham was older. (The family get togethers must have been full of fascinating memories.) Abraham entered Canaan 430 years after the flood.

You might be dizzy from reading all the numbers. Or confused because you have noticed the evolutionary timeline and the biblical timeline do not match. The Jemdat Nasr Period dates to 3000 BC. But Dr. Osgood is saying it fits to Abraham and nearer to 1950 BC.

Here is the solution: evolution's timeline is packed with empty years and huge gaps, thousands and millions of years, where nothing happens. You cannot place biblical events on this timeline and expect it to make sense.

The Bible insists man's history is about six thousand years so far. Creation happened around 4000 BC; the flood happened around 2348 BC, and according to the genealogies in Genesis, there are approximately 352 years between the flood and Abraham's birth.

Scholars begin dating civilization and language around 5000 BC and do not acknowledge that these people are the first people after

---

[2] Other respected Creationists follow the LXX version which adds or subtracts years from the list in Genesis 5. A known error has Methuselah living 14 yrs after the flood. We are using the Masoretic Text as further investigation is needed into the differences of the LXX.

Noah's flood, 2348 BC and after. They date the Uruk Expansion out of southern Iraq around 4000 BC, but do not recognize it as the movement of people after the Tower of Babel in 2242 BC, the biblical date. Some people think discoveries dating to 5000 BC are people of the flood. Most creationists believe nothing would have survived such a catastrophe, ruined cities included.

So, to review, according to the Ebla Tablets, Abraham was going into Canaan during the Old Kingdoms in Egypt or just before, and the Early Dynastic Period in Sumeria, perhaps before Sargon the Great reigned, before Dynasty III, and during what is traditionally called the Early Bronze Age 1. Dr. Osgood places Abraham nearer the Jemdat Nasr Period. And, according to Osgood, a thousand years could be shaved off the traditional timeline.[3]

Here are a few other things to remember about the dates. The biblical timeline for the Old Kingdom in Egypt and the Early Dynastic periods in Mesopotamia fit around Abraham's lifetime. Evolutionists, on the other hand, consider the first civilizations began emerging around 5000 BC. But, according to the Bible it was after 2348 BC, and it didn't take long to see city and kingdom building. Evolution is the biggest fly in the soup when it comes to dating history and ignoring the Bible.

The farthest biblically you can go back is around 4000 years before Christ. The flood happened about two thousand years after creation, and a little over four hundred years after the flood, Abraham was going to Canaan. There were no empty times in man's history when he was banging rocks together mindlessly and grunting into his beard because he didn't know how to talk.

Besides pushing back Abraham's life into the time of the Old Kingdom era of Egypt, the Ebla Tablets disprove the theory of those scholars

---

[3] Osgood, "The Times of Abraham."

who thought Terah wanted to move to Canaan because Sumer was in a dark age. The dark age of Sumer happened after Abraham moved.

So what was going on at the time of Abraham in Mesopotamia?

War and trade. And war because of trade. Mesopotamia experienced wars between city states almost as soon as there were city-states after the flood. One of the earliest known wars dates to the Ubaid people and the Uruk Expansion at Hamoukar in northeast Syria near its border with Iraq and Turkey.[4]

Hamoukar surprised archaeologists when they discovered it was an obsidian tool manufacturing site. A tool factory? Thousands of clay bullets for slings were found there. Someone wanted rights to the obsidian perhaps. Of course, people had always been fighting and killing each other since Cain and Abel, in a city or outside of it. They fought over land, goods and gods—the same things people fight over today.

If Terah had a reason besides God's conversation with Abraham, war may have been Terah's catalyst for moving. Skirmishes in Mesopotamia could be large or small. A battle may have been why Haran died young. Canaan, seemingly out of the reach of greedy kings, may have looked good to Terah.

Remember the scholars who believe Abraham and Terah were traveling merchants? They believe money was the reason Terah wanted to move. But he never made it to Canaan because Harran was a big city, poised at a crossroads and an excellent place to do business. In a setting like Harran, people came to him. How could he lose? Others think Terah made idols. Harran was a good place for that trade as well.

Some think it was famine that pushed Terah out of Ur. Archaeologist Harvey Weiss believed he uncovered evidence of an extended

---

[4] William Harms, "Evidence of battle at Hamoukar points to early urban development," (*The University of Chicago Chronicle* Vol. 26 No.8 2007).

drought at Tell Leilan, the ancient city of Shekhna.[5] The site is about thirty miles east of Urkesh. He dated the city to 5000 BC, and said it was abandoned because of drought around 1726 BC. This drought may not fit with the biblical timing for Abraham, however.

If you get a chance, you might like to read an ancient poem called the *Curse of Akkad*. Naram-Sin, Sargon's grandson, was blamed for the drought. He attacked a temple and toppled the god who just happened to control the weather. The drought was Naram-Sin's punishment.

While the ancients blamed a god for the drought, Harvey Weiss and other scientists blamed global warming and climate shifts. Actually, there are many scientists saying the demise of civilizations was all caused by climate changes.

We cannot say climate change was why Terah wanted to move to Canaan, however. War or economic opportunities are better choices, that is if you don't think he was influenced by Abraham's mission. But Terah never made it to Canaan. All we can say about that truthfully is he didn't make it because he changed his mind and didn't want to, or he wasn't able to because of his health. He died in Harran.

We do not know if he left earth trusting God or clutching his idols. According to Joshua 24:2, it was the latter. Which seems surprising when we know Shem, his seventh great grandfather, was still alive and giving his testimony of the true God. Families have always been families, is the lesson here, made up of members who choose God and those who do not.

But one day Abraham woke up in Harran and God appeared to him again. This time Abraham had no one to delay him. His father was dead. He was in charge of his own life. When it looked like Abraham

---

[5] Harvey Weiss, "Revising the contours of history at Tell Leilan," *Annales Archéologiques Arabes Syriennes*, 45-46, 59-74.

was firmly established and growing his holdings in Harran, God said leave everything behind. God had a different plan that involved making Abraham more than he thought possible.

Abraham packed his belongings. Genesis 12:5 says, "And Abram took Sarai his wife, and Lot his brother's son, and all their substance that they had gathered, and the souls that they had gotten in Harran."

You might have noticed, he took things he wasn't supposed to again, like Lot. And, it sounds like Abraham had slaves. Slavery did exist during Abraham's lifetime throughout Mesopotamia and beyond. This wasn't a slavery based on skin color; it happened to people who lost their freedom because they were kidnapped or conquered in war, or not able to pay off debt to a debt collector. Some people sold themselves into slavery. Some sold their children. During a famine, a child could be sold into slavery so it could be fed. Criminals could be made slaves as punishment. Foreigners were especially targeted for involuntary slavery.

But slavery in ancient times was not always a matter of one person owning another. It could be a contract between two people on a work agreement. The tenure could be short or it could be for life. This type of slave was protected by laws and had rights. Raymond Westbrook in his article in the *Chicago-Kent Law Review* sites many examples of this from the Ebla and Nuzi Tablets.

Harsh treatment, however, was a reality for many slaves who could not pay the contracted redemption price. If they couldn't pay, the slave fell lower in status, like a criminal slave. These slaves were marked with tattoos, like on a shaven head for example. Some wore a special pierced ear tag. This piercing differed from the common pierced ears of women and men during the time period. These slaves could be legally mistreated within certain guidelines. We call this group chattel slaves.

But debt slaves or other slaves were treated as employees, and debt slavery was limited to a number of years. Slaves could potentially marry another slave or a free person, own property, conduct business and buy their freedom. To us, this class of slavery was not the ideal life either, but for the poor, it may have been better than starving.

Abraham as a foreigner outside of his homeland was vulnerable himself. But as a slave owner, he must not have been a harsh master. While he was in Canaan, living as a nomad and a foreigner, he had hundreds of people working for him. They outnumbered him. They could have run away into the wilderness, but they didn't. They chose to stay with him. And, fight in a war for him. One slave was in a position to inherit everything Abraham owned.

Abraham did not seem to possess a harsh character. He had submitted to his father's needs to stay in Harran, had not taken a second wife because his first one couldn't have children and had assumed responsibility for his brother's son. We might conclude the slaves in Abraham's possession were not as bad off as slaves of another master.

If they were slaves. Jewish scholars teach Abraham was preaching about the city whose builder and maker is God (Hebrews 11:10), and people wanted to travel with him. But the word translated souls is *nephesh* (NEHfesh) and includes any breathing creature which can also mean animals. It must be admitted, however, if this verse isn't talking about servants, he was given some in Egypt.

Genesis 12:5 also reveals Abraham did not correct his first mistake about obeying God. Lot was included in the people Abraham packed up to travel with him. He did not understand he was making a mistake. It was a great opportunity for Lot, and Abraham probably wanted his help.

The easiest way to Canaan was to travel the trade routes. Scholars have Abraham traveling south out of Harran, crossing the Euphrates and passing Aleppo, Ebla and Damascus. Then he would have continued south and crossed into Canaan through the Golan Heights on a route connecting to the Way of the Philistines.

If Abraham did travel that way, he turned south onto a side route leading to Shechem. Shechem was a major trade city in Canaan by the time Abraham's grandson, Jacob, visited it in Genesis 33. It was a city with walls and gates. The Stele of Khu-Sebek talks about a visit to *Sekmem* that resulted in a battle with "Asiatics."[6] Khu-Sebek was a nobleman during the reign of Sesostris III. Asiatics were Semites.

But Abraham didn't mention a city. He described a place called the oak of Moreh. "And Abram passed through the land unto the place of Sichem, unto the plain of Moreh." (Genesis 12:6) Plain is the word *'êlôn* (ayLONE) and means an oak or a strong, great tree and plain. The picture is a large tree on a plain.

Even though the scholars who favor the northern crossing into Canaan have good reasons for choosing that way, there may be biblical evidence supporting a different entrance. In Genesis 31-33 we are given a travel itinerary for Jacob's return to Canaan from the area of Harran. The mountains of Gilead are mentioned, Mahanaim, Penuel and the Jabbok River. All these locations are east of the Jordan River.

It was a route south from Damascus through the valleys east of the Jordan River. By crossing the Jordan in between the mountains of Ebal and Gerizim, Jacob arrived at Shechem. Jacob made this trip with flocks, herds, servants and family. His father-in-law caught up to him at Gilead in seven days. This may have been the route Abraham had taken. Abraham too had "all their substance that they had gathered." (Genesis 12:5) This wasn't a roadtrip with a couple goats for milking and a handful of sheep and fowl for food. It was the entire household with everything they owned.

---

[6] Campbell Price, Texts in Translation #13: The Stela of Sobek-khu (Acc. no. 3306)

Abraham could have brought camels. The two-humped variety was a northern beast of burden. Ox carts were also in use. There were shepherds, servants and enough animals to feed and clothe everyone, tents and their hardware, mats, cups, pots, pitchers, vessels, oil, grains for bread, hand-sized grinding stones and whatever else made up the kitchen. Lots of stuff. Traveling along rivers provided water and fertile valleys fed the livestock.

If Abraham's entrance into Canaan was through the pass between Mt. Ebal and Mt. Gerizim, it must have felt dramatic. We said Abraham did not mention the city. Excavations at Shechem discovered why he didn't. The city, fifteen acres with strong walls, was not built yet.

Even though Abraham did not describe it, the Ebla Tablets talk about Shechem and its god Resheph. Tell Balata in the West Bank is the traditional site for ancient Shechem and is named for the Arabaic city constructed on top of it. It is thirty miles north of Jerusalem and slightly southeast of Nablus. Perched in an east west valley between the two mountains, Shechem was an intersection for trade routes heading north, south, east and west.

Abraham noted its tree, a great tree growing on the plain of Moreh. Scholars believe this tree was special. The Hebrew language indicates it was strong. Some think it may have been growing for some time, one of the first trees to sprout after the flood. Moreh in Hebrew can mean teacher or early rain, and its root word means one who shoots an arrow.

Some think this may have been a pagan worship site. Others think Moreh may have been a man's name, since people were living there. The Bible says Hivites lived there. But it was on this land, near this tree, that God appeared to Abraham again. "And the LORD appeared unto Abram, and said, Unto thy seed will I give this land." (Genesis 12:7)

Was this Jesus? Scholars and commentators say yes. Here at

Shechem, God fulfilled His promise to show Abraham the land. Abraham built an altar to God there. "And there builded he an altar unto the LORD, who appeared unto him."

This place was not a random location in Canaan. It was where Abraham was led. In a sense, it was the belly of the land. The tree was a landmark, and it became a landmark of faith for the Israelites.

About two hundred years later, Abraham's grandson Jacob (Israel) would return to Shechem, then a fortified city. He bought ground there and pitched his tent. A little north of the city, he dug a well that you can visit today in the Church of St. Photina.

Like Abraham, Jacob built an altar too, naming it "Elelohe-Israel," the mighty God of Israel. (Genesis 33:20) Jacob made the people with him surrender their idols, and he buried the idols under the tree in Shechem to purify his household. (Genesis 35:4) He declared that his son Joseph should inherit the land he had bought there. But Joseph's brothers sold him to slave traders passing through Shechem instead.

While Jacob was living near Shechem, his daughter was attacked by the crown prince. The prince wanted to marry her, and the king came to make a deal with Jacob. But Jacob's sons were angry that the prince had mistreated their sister. They pretended to be friendly and then killed all the men of Shechem.

In 1406 BC Joshua brought the Israelites to Shechem. He brought them again before he died. He stood on the ground Abraham had stood, on the ground Jacob had stood, on the ground Joseph had stood, and with the two mountains as his witness, commanded the Israelites to choose whom they were going to serve: God or idols. Joshua reminded them of Terah and Nahor's idols and the false gods of Canaan. (Joshua 8 and 24)

But there is no record, biblical or archaeological for the Israelite take over of Shechem. Dr. David G. Hansen thinks there may be evidence in Joshua 8, however, that shows them listening to Joshua read the law. Perhaps they surrendered willingly after hearing about Ai. One of the Amarna Letters seems to support the theory. Shechem's King Labaya was scorned for giving the city (Sakmu) to the habiru. "Are we to act like Lab'ayu when he was giving the land of Sakmu to the Hapiru?"[7] However it happened, Shechem became a city of refuge in Israel.

Joshua and the Israelites buried Joseph's bones at Shechem. Just like Jacob, they were returning to the land promised them by visiting Abraham's first landmark. Today Palestinian authorities control Joseph's tomb. In 2000 it was ransacked. In 2015 it was burned in a riot.

The book of Judges tells us Gideon rescued Shechem from the Midianites. His son became the first king of Israel there, but it ended in the destruction of the city. Later, Shechem was the first capital of the Northern Kingdom under Jeroboam.

Even Jesus visited Shechem when He spoke with the Samaritan woman at the well. It was a scheduled visit on God's agenda. Shechem was Abraham's first stop in Canaan. It was the place where God declared Himself faithful to Abraham, promising to give him the land and bless him, and the place Jesus declared He was the Anointed One.

But it became a place of Israel's deceit and a witness to their unfaithfulness. Jesus came and sat with a wayward, despised Samaritan, an image of unfaithfulness. But to this woman, in that place He openly proclaimed Himself as the Messiah.

When Abraham built his altar in Shechem, he was declaring his allegiance to the God who was revealing Himself to him. He was choosing the authority in his life and was showing an outward sign of the trust of God growing inside him. Abraham was willing to plant that

---

[7] William L. Moran, *The Amttrna Letters*, (London:The Johns Hopkins Press Ltd.1992) EA 290.

sign like a flag marking God's words to him, and his descendants understood the importance of his actions.

Abraham did not stay in Shechem like Terah had stayed in Harran. "And he removed from thence unto a mountain on the east of Bethel, and pitched his tent, having Bethel on the west, and Hai on the east: and there he builded an altar unto the LORD, and called upon the name of the LORD." (Genesis 12:8)

Ancient Bethel, House of God, was originally a town named Luz. According to recent research it is near El Bireh today. Ai was near it, probably Khirbet el-Maqatir.[8] It was an uphill journey for Abraham to go to Luz, and with animals it probably took a few days. He pitched his tent between these two Canaanite cities and built another altar.

At this altar, he began calling on the name of the Lord. Calling is *qârâ'* (kuhRAH), to cry, to call out to, to proclaim. Abraham didn't wait for God to appear to him; he called out using the name *Yhôvâh*, Jehovah. There in the middle ground between two Canaanite cities, Abraham began to worship God and proclaim His name to his family and the people he had brought from Harran.

It was a location with a great view of the surrounding land, land God promised would someday belong to Abraham's family. We do not know how many tents Abraham needed to shelter his crew, but we may know what the tents looked like. According to the Ancient Hebrew Research Center, they were black and made out of goat hair. The tents could be large, with black roofs and separate, lighter colored side pieces. The side pieces could be raised to let in the breeze or lowered for privacy and shelter.

The black roof of the tent provided shade from the intense sun,

---

[8] Scott Stripling and Mark Hassler, "Biblical City Of Ai Located," Patterns of Evidence, Feb.9, 2019.

but also retained heat for cooler nights. The goat hair was woven to create sections that were stretched over sturdy poles. The hair swelled when it got wet, making a rain-proof barrier. Mats or old goat hair panels covered the floor of the two main rooms inside the tent.

The tents were arranged in a sprawling circle. This arrangement created a wall to the outside, and in the Hebrew language the camp was a place of strength, healing, love, comfort, refuge and rescue. The word camp is related to the word grace.[9] So began Abraham's new life in Canaan as one who lived in tents.

He never moved into a town like some of the Amorite nomads we learned about, leaving their servants in the tent camps to watch the flocks and herds. Abraham said he lived in Canaan as a sojourner. (Genesis 23:4) *Tôshâb* (toeSHAV) is the word translated sojourner, and it means a temporary inmate, a person dwelling as a foreigner in a country where he is not a naturalized citizen. In English a sojourn is a temporary stay.

This is how Abraham thought about himself living in Canaan. God was going to give Abraham the land of Canaan, yes, but through his descendants. Abraham must have wondered at this. Every morning as he stepped from his tent to meet the view from his highland camp, he may have said to himself, "Jehovah is giving this to me." Yet he knew the possessing of his promise was for a future time.

We know the history of his descendants. We know the story of their rise to power. For Abraham it was a dream like a mirage. But he began to be obedient to what his mind could grasp. He started worshipping God. He started talking about God, and he separated himself from the culture

---

[9] Jeff A. Benner, "The meaning of Grace from a Hebrew perspective," Ancient Hebrew Research Center.

oozing out of the cities around him. He spoke a similar language. He lived a similar lifestyle as those of the countryside. But he began to build a life on a different religious foundation than his father. He had chosen the authority speaking into his life, and he wasn't turning back.

Canaan doesn't have a good reputation according to the Bible. It was called the land of milk and honey, but its people were called wicked, its religion detestable. Its cities were listed on tablets at Ebla, but scholars knew nothing about Canaanite culture until 1928.

About half a mile from the Mediterranean coast in Ras Shamra, Syria, a farmer plowing his field thought he had hit a rock. When he looked, he found a large hole instead. A year later the first important Canaanite tablets were found at Ras Shamra. Three years later, scholars were able to decipher the new alphabet and identify it as a Semitic language related to Hebrew.

By accident the farmer had found the city of Ugarit. It was an important trade city southwest of Ebla with connections to the Hittites, Egyptians and the island of Cyprus. The lowest and earliest (6000 BC) levels of excavations show people had arrived from Iraq and northwest Mesopotamia. There is evidence of the Halaf and Ubaid cultures in the first settlements. In the top levels of excavations, Mesopotamian and Hittite influences are seen, until the Amorite culture took hold in the Second Millennium BC, the topmost layer.

Even then, however, there is a strong Greek influence. Ugarit was a city with a diverse population as might be expected in a city of merchants. Scribes wrote in four languages to record events. Since evidence of Merneptah is the last pharaoh found at Ugarit, it is assumed the city was destroyed during or after his reign. Scholars date this to the time of Israel's judges. Most agree Ugarit was destroyed by the time of Ramesses III.

The Ras Shamra excavations tell us Ugarit existed when Abraham entered Canaan. He had surely heard of the place. But its height of power happened later, just as the Bible says. What scholars have learned from Ugarit about Canaanite culture echoes its biblical description.

The Ugarit texts reveal a sexually perverse society founded on a sexually perverse religion. Fertility cults with prostitutes serving as priests and priestesses were a major part of the religion. People sold their children into prostitution, homosexual and heterosexual. Rape was common activity among the gods. There were other sexually deviant practices also. The values of the religion were the values of the people who invented it.

Child sacrifice was another widespread practice. At Carthage, where the Canaanite religion had influence, more than 20,000 infants' burnt remains were discovered. Older children ages four-six could also be sacrificed. Children were placed on the outstretched arms of the god statue and rolled into the fire. Plutarch described music loud enough to drown out a baby's screams.[10]

Beginning in 1970, the acceptance of the evidence for child sacrifice in ancient history waned. But recent research has confirmed the practice, and new discoveries were made in Turkey.[11]

The gods of Canaan were El, Asherah, Baal, Molech, Mot, Anath, Dagon and many more. These perverse gods were violent and murderous, with no respect for life. El is a Semitic name for God, but the El of Canaan had nothing in common with the Jehovah of Abraham. Asherah is considered El's wife or sister or both. Later in Israel's history, when they were worshipping the gods of Canaan, the Israelites joined

---

[10] Clay Jones, "The Horror of Canaanite Children's 'Family' Life," Clay Jones.

[11] Robin Ngo, "Did the Carthaginians Really Practice Infant Sacrifice?" *Bible History Daily*, April 2, 2018.

Asherah with Yahweh. It was blasphemy.

But these practices had not reached their full measure when Abraham lived in Canaan. Still, you can see why Abraham remained separate from the main culture there. Steadily he was staking out his own culture based on the values of the one true God who appeared to him.

Some scholars like to say Abraham was the first to begin a monotheistic religion. That is not true. How many gods did Adam talk to in the Garden of Eden? How many did he walk with? How many gods did Abel worship with his sacrifices in Genesis 4? How many gods did Methuselah and Noah worship? What about Melchizedek, the priest of the Most High God in Genesis 14?

Monotheism, the belief and worship of one God, existed long before Abraham built his altars in Canaan. Abraham was the first to make monotheism a national religion, however, through his grandson Jacob. But his religion wasn't in a new god. It was the continuing revelation of the only God, the one who had created Adam, the one whom Abel, Methuselah, Noah and Melchizedek worshipped.

Judaism, Christianity and Islam are said to be the three monotheistic religions that came from Abraham. But only two can be connected to Abraham: Judaism and Christianity. Many people view these as two separate religions. The Christian Church, however, has Judaism as its foundation and is the continuing revelation of Abraham's faith and Moses' laws. When Jesus returns, both will be fully realized in Him.

Islam came hundreds of years after the Church began, thousands after Judaism. Abraham's oldest son Ishmael was not a Muslim. Neither were his children by Keturah. In fact, the *shasu* of YWH inscription we talked about earlier points to the regions where these children would have lived. Their descendants knew the name of the God Abraham worshipped.

The Islamic Allah is not Jehovah of the Jewish or Christian religion.

When the Jews and Christians told Muhammad that, it started a war.[12] Abraham may be a flesh and blood ancestor to some Islamic people, but he is not a spiritual father. Abraham never worshipped a god like Allah.

That is why it is confusing to Jews and Christians that Muslims claim Jacob's well, Abraham's *Jewish* grandson's well, as a holy site. Or Ezekiel's tomb, Joseph's tomb, Bethlehem, and Jerusalem, all distinctly Jewish sites. But the Islamic faith has written alternative stories for those ancient Jewish believers and their cities to Islamicize them.

And Abraham was Semitic, so to be anti-Semitic is to be anti-Abrahamic. This is also confusing to Jews because if one claims Abraham as a father, he must be partly Semitic too. The anti-Semitism in the Middle East elevates the relationship to Abraham's concubines, Hagar and Keturah, and minimizes Abraham's true faith and heritage.

Surrounded by the false gods of Canaan, Abraham's trust in Yahweh only grew stronger. But Abraham didn't stay in Bethel either. He continued his journey south to the Negev (NEHgav). Negev means south or southward and comes from a root that means parched. It is a high, rocky desert even though during winter rains it blooms. Rugged and beautiful, the northern reaches were used for grazing from antiquity.

But it soon became clear Abraham had a problem. A famine had struck the area. "And there was a famine in the land: and Abram went down into Egypt to sojourn there; for the famine was grievous in the land." (Genesis 12:10)

Soon after he arrived in Canaan, a deadly obstacle arose to threaten failure. Occasional famines plagued Canaan in the Old Testament. Three are recorded in Genesis. Some were severe. The one during Joseph's lifetime stretched as far south as Egypt and lasted for seven years. Isaac witnessed a drought in which he was supernaturally blessed. Elijah's lasted three years.

---

[12] To learn more read *Countries in the Bible: Who They Are Today* by Flying Eagle Publications.

With all this talk of drought, and images of sparse grasslands in the Holy Land, you might wonder how the numbers of large flocks and herds listed in the Bible could survive.

Dr. Brian Thomas states archaeological finds have shown the ancient Middle East had a wetter climate. Andrew Garrard and others excavated the Azraq Basin in Jordan and discovered the remains of an ancient lake. Thomas states their discoveries fit better with the accounts in the Old Testament than they do with evolutionary theories.

Archaeologists have also discovered the Arabian and Sahara deserts were not the dry wastelands we see today. A group of scientists who studied rainfall models and published their results in a Royal Society journal concluded the ancient Middle East was wetter than it is today. This research contradicts the opinions of climate change scholars who declared it suffered prolonged drought.

But it seems science agrees with the Bible that the land was capable of sustaining large flocks and herds. Abraham, however, was facing a severe drought. Thankfully, Egypt did not always experience the same drought patterns as Canaan.

Abraham went to Egypt and some scholars think he may have visited as early as the First or Fourth Dynasty. If he visited in the Fourth, it was a time of relative peace. Dynasties Five and Six were similar, focused on trade and growing the Egyptian religion. It was also the time true pyramids were constructed.

Since Abraham had lived in Ur, he may have felt at home in the grandeur of an Egyptian city. But it was in Egypt one of his biggest fears was realized. Genesis 20:13 says Abraham had asked his wife Sarai for a favor before they left Harran. "This is thy kindness which thou shalt shew unto me; at every place whither we shall come, say of me, He is my brother."

He wasn't asking her to lie, exactly. She was his half sister. Abraham said they had the same father, Terah, but different mothers. Modern readers need to remember that marrying your sibling wasn't considered illegal, and weird, until after God established Israel's laws during Moses' lifetime.

We do not know if Abraham was handsome. Sarah, on the other hand, was beautiful. Abraham thought so and so did a few men. It wasn't an issue before, but Abraham was expecting it was going to be.

He knew his life was in danger because they would kill him to take her. It was illegal to sleep with another man's wife. But it was possible to eliminate the husband. He was a foreigner, especially vulnerable. Laws did not necessarily apply to him. Lawless conduct against visitors may be seen in Genesis 19 or Judges 19.

And, he and Sarah were coming into Egypt for their own benefit, to survive a famine. The Egyptians would expect something in return for sharing their resources. Foreigners would be considered on the level of slaves. The Egyptians wouldn't kill Sarah. Men would want her. Abraham knew if he were killed, she would be completely alone, and what might happen to her if they tired of her?

A brother, however, was a different matter than a husband. Men would be nice to him because they liked his sister. In the ancient Middle East, and even in some places today, an interested suitor didn't court the woman; they courted her father or brother.

Abraham repeated his request to Sarah just before they entered Egypt. She understood her fate. It was a risk to her own safety, but it would keep Abraham alive, and alive was better than dead and she alone. She was in her sixties; for her, middle-aged, a fact skeptics think makes the story unbelievable. Unbelievable or not, her beauty got them into trouble twice.

Abraham's plan seemed like a good idea. All he had to do was hold out long enough, and then he and Sarah could leave Egypt and go back to Canaan. He may have never intended on putting her in danger. But he probably didn't expect to have to deal with the Pharaoh either.

We can only guess how long Abraham was in Egypt before the nobles saw Sarah and told the king of her beauty. It may have been a casual interest at first, a casual inquiry. Perhaps the nobles were seeking to improve their standing with the king by keeping their eye out for potential wives. Perhaps they tired of Abraham's passive delays. Finally Pharaoh commanded the nobles to take her to be one of his wives.

Sarah was kidnapped. The word taken is *lâqach (luhKACKH)* and contains the meaning of being seized or carried away. The pharaoh did pay Abraham well, but it wasn't a deal Abraham could refuse. It looked like Abraham messed up the promise God made to him.

*A*braham closed his eyes against the chaos swirling around him. Bleating sheep and goats, braying donkeys and the anxious bellowing of the oxen drowned the questions of his new servants.

The smell, the noise, the dust sickened him and faded away upon the memory of Sarai's frightened face as she was torn from him. His heart pounded in his chest. His dazed mind threw thoughts at him wildly.

Terah's scorn. Nahor's indifference. The promise. Finally Shechem. The drought. "We must take her now!"

"God, is this your idea of blessing?"

Say you are my sister...

What he had feared was happening. Had the promise ended before it had begun? Or had it already evaporated in the drought?

Abram opened his eyes. Lot's face was white. He had torn his robe. A young girl, an Egyptian, looked up at him. Her eyes were as frightened as Sarai's had been.

He looked toward the palace. The maid had nothing to worry about. He only hoped Sarai didn't either.

Chapter 4
The Egypt Incident

Abraham doesn't say if he had asked God what to do about having a gorgeous wife. It seems as if he invented the she-is-my-sister plan himself. To be fair to Abraham, however, it was God who suggested to Samuel how to sidestep around King Saul (1Samuel 16:2). If those Egyptians could have been relied upon to behave morally, to treat people with respect, or if he would have been further along in his faith, Abraham may never have resorted to deceit.

We do not know if Abraham protested as Pharaoh's men seized Sarah. We do not know his thoughts as animals and servants were brought to add to his stock to pay for her. What animals Pharaoh gave and in what quantities are not known, but apparently Pharaoh thought she was a valuable enough that he needed to compensate Abraham.

Thankfully God thought she was valuable too. Women never had it easy in the ancient world. But God has never abandoned his daughters…or sons even when they made mistakes.

Imagine Sarah's thoughts as Abraham reminded her of their vulnerability among foreigners in a foreign land. There was no Israeli Embassy in Egypt then. Foreign individuals had no diplomat to represent them. They were not protected by a set of laws, and if there were any laws, the king could choose not to abide by them. There was no ruler sitting on a throne back home to send a rescuer.

It is notable that Sarah is referred to as "the woman" in Egypt. She had lost her identity. She had been reduced to flesh, in the eyes of her husband and in the eyes of the Egyptians.

She may have felt abandoned, by her brother and God. She had not borne any children to Abraham. Here she was, sixty-five, a good looking but useless wife according to the traditions and purpose of marriage in Mesopotamia. As a pharaoh's concubine, her main purpose, the expectation, was not primarily to produce children. It was to provide pleasure and boasting rights. If the Pharaoh tired of her, she could be thrown out into the streets, given away, whatever he decided.

Was God casting her aside? Had he chosen someone for Abraham who was more capable? Was she tempted by the luxuries of Egypt in Pharaoh's harem? None of Sarah's thoughts in Egypt are recorded for us. We only imagine the fears assaulting her mind.

But 1Peter 3:6 tells us Sarah did not surrender to her fears. She had no legal papers, no earthly ruler and no relative to help her. Who she did have on her side was God.

Scholars ponder her immediate fate. Some like to think she was taken into a harem and was being prepared for Pharaoh like Esther was for her king. But the Bible does not say that. We do not know how long she was in Pharaoh's house. The Bible says nothing of their encounter.

Or does it?

Scholars recite Pharaoh's conversation with Abraham in Genesis 12:19, "And so I took her for my wife," and some say Pharaoh did have relations with Sarah and some say he didn't. But there is an interesting twist in Genesis 12:17. *Green's Literal Translation* states, "And Jehovah touched Pharaoh and his house with great plagues on the word of Sarai, Abram's wife."

'*Al* is the Hebrew word for because of, upon, for, through. *Dâbâr* (duhVAR) means word or a matter or affair. Jewish rabbis note the wording— because of the word, upon the word— and translate it on account of, but they interpret a conversation either between Sarah and Pharaoh or Sarah and God.[1]

Perhaps Sarah called on God to save her from Pharaoh. Perhaps she told the truth and warned Pharaoh of disaster if he sinned against her because she was a married woman. All we know by the verse is she feared God. Somehow, either before or after a visit with Sarah, Pharaoh and his household, which may have included those nobles who discovered her, were afflicted with a terrible plague.

We cannot identify the plague, but the fact that it was great impressed Pharaoh to listen to Sarah. He quickly summoned Abraham. Do you hear the indignant anger in Pharaoh's words? "What is this that you have done to me? Why didn't you tell me that she was your wife? Why did you say, 'She is my sister,' so that I took her to be my wife?" (Genesis 12:18-19 WEB)

We find out later in Genesis 20 that Sarah and Abraham have the same father but not the same mother. Some scholars insist she is Abraham's niece, Iscah, since he calls Lot his brother in Genesis 13:8. But the word used for brother is '*âch* and it can also mean kindred. Abraham may have been referring to a general condition of family in the passage about Lot. Or, Sarah and Lot really were siblings.

It is interesting that Genesis 11:26 doesn't say Terah had other sons or daughters. You might think it would be written down if Sarah was

---

[1] Dr. Gabriel H. Kohn, "Say You Are My Sister," Department of Bible Bar-Ilan University's Parashat Hashavua Study Center Parashat Lekh Lekha 5765/ October 23, 2004.

a daughter. Instead, Sarah is called his daughter-in-law and is referred to as Abraham's bride and spouse. The Hebrew word *'ab* (av) means father, but it can mean forefather and even grandfather. This may give support to the idea of Sarah being Terah's granddaughter, Abraham's niece, Iscah, since she is never mentioned again. It could be the Bible's way of telling us Sarai and Iscah are the same person.

This might be why it is pointed out in the verses that Abraham asked Sarah to say she was his sister, to take advantage of their blood relation to Terah as an avenue of protection. Sarah's background seems a mystery to us, and some wonder why Moses would not have given it since she was the mother of the Israelites (and all those of faith). But the truth may be it is plain; we just don't understand it.

Another claim some make is Abraham adopted Sarah as his sister to give her protection and a higher status in the culture. This practice was found in the Nuzi Tablets. A man could have two documents made, one to establish a woman as his wife and another to establish the same woman as his sister. We cannot assume he did this by his words, however.

Abraham defined their relationship in Genesis 20:12. "... she is my sister; she is the daughter of my father, but not the daughter of my mother; and she became my wife."

Another interesting possibility shown in the Nuzi Tablets and Old Babylonian law codes is that a man could adopt a girl as a daughter and daughter-in-law.[2] This arrangement was formed by contract and usually provided for the woman to stay in the aging man's house to care for him until death and to be married to his son. Could this be the reason Abraham did not leave Terah behind? Was Sarah contracted to care for him? Fascinating, but we cannot assume that either.

---

[2]Dr. Robert Paulissian "Adoption in Ancient Assyria and Babylonia." *Journal of Assyrian Academic Studies* Volume 13 No. 2 pg 21-22

Abimelech (ahBEE MELeck) was a Philistine king who also admired Sarah and desired to have her as his wife— thirty years after her incident with Pharaoh. Sarah was ninety in Genesis 20! Again Sarah was taken by force, but this king sent nothing to Abraham as payment. In his one defense, Abimelech asked Sarah if Abraham was her brother, and she said that he was. Perhaps she feared this king would kill Abraham.

But again God intervened by warning Abimelech, and we learn of his partial innocence before God. Partial because he did steal her.

> But God came to Abimelech in a dream by night, and said to him, Behold, thou art but a dead man, for the woman which thou hast taken; for she is a man's wife. But Abimelech had not come near her: and he said, Lord, wilt thou slay also a righteous nation? Said he not unto me, She is my sister? and she, even she herself said, He is my brother: in the integrity of my heart and innocency of my hands have I done this. And God said unto him in a dream, Yea, I know that thou didst this in the integrity of thy heart; for I also withheld thee from sinning against me. (Genesis 20:3-6)

The Philistine also loaded Abraham with gifts after his encounter with God. He even consulted Sarah and specifically gave her a thousand pieces of silver. But Pharaoh didn't heed any warnings if he got them. He was given a plague. Notice Pharaoh never asked Abraham to return the gifts. Instead he gave Abraham a royal escort out of Egypt.

Abraham's deceit concerning these two kings has been scrutinized, criticized and spiritualized for centuries. The same for his treatment of Sarah. God said nothing to reprimand either Abraham or Sarah. One lesson everyone learned in Egypt and Canaan was Abraham's God was powerful, and He was Abraham's and Sarah's protector. Abraham's and Sarah's trust must have grown when they learned they could depend on Him. For those born later, the incident in Egypt was a shadow of the captivity, plagues and exodus of the Israelites.

The Bible doesn't say if the drought in Canaan was over when Abraham and Sarah left Egypt. But the drought, if it was still happening, may have seemed like a lesser threat than Egypt. Really, if God could rescue them out of Pharaoh's hand, what was drought? They must have left with thankful, amazed hearts.

The Bible says they went up out of Egypt. "And Abram went up out of Egypt, he, and his wife, and all that he had, and Lot with him, into the south." (Genesis 13:1) The area of the Negev lay north of Egypt. If you remember, we learned Negev means south. Abraham wasn't confused. He was traveling north but called it the south, the southern end of the land he was to inherit.

And it was an uphill climb. From the Nile Delta, the land rises as it reaches Canaan. Craggy peaks along the Sinai border with Israel level out as you travel north. The Negev forms a natural boundary out of Israel with its ridges running east to west rising higher and higher as you first cross one level then climb to the next. So, mountains really do surround Israel.

Leopards roamed this wilderness, hunting ibex, hyrax and domesticated livestock. Arabian leopards are the smallest in the world. Ancient stone leopard traps were found in the Negev which experts date to the time of Abraham and even before.

Other wild animals made the rocks and desert their home too. Hyenas, jackals, wolves, onagers, gazelles, antelopes, the Arabian oryx, cheetahs and Asiatic lions lived there.

One of the unique features of the Negev are closed valleys caused by extreme water erosion. We might be tempted to call them craters surrounded by steep rock walls like a box canyon, but Israelis have named them the *makhteshim* which means mortars. There are five of these formations in the Negev. In their book, *The Makhteshim Country*, Emanuel Mazor and Boris Krasnov call them geological windows.[3]

Once past the craggy heights, the Negev settles into plains in the central region. There, sandstone hills, canyons and wadis can flood during torrential rains. It can be dangerous. In 2018, ten Israeli teens drowned in a flash flood as a ten foot wave overcame them while hiking.

The Negev covers about half of modern Israel, and is the one desert in the world decreasing in size because Israel uses water conservation, water filtration and drought tolerant crops to make it bloom.

Temperatures in the most southern area can reach over 100°F in summer and receives about an inch of rainfall. Near Beersheba *(Be'ersheva)*, in the central part where Abraham and Isaac lived, rainfall is about eight inches a year and summer temperatures are a little over 90°F.

The trip up out of Egypt wasn't a quick jaunt. Abraham came out of Egypt with more possessions than when he entered. His entourage may have been as big or bigger than the merchants traveling the east west trade routes through the Negev. He may have been carrying as much silver and gold too.

We said some scholars think Abraham engaged in the merchant trade. He probably had good opportunities to do so, but he was not the traveling Amorite salesman they portray. What they don't believe is that he had camels. In the list of animals Abraham owned, camels are included. These camels may have been ones he brought with him from Ur or perhaps they were given to him by Pharaoh.

---

[3] Krasnov, Boris and Emanuel Mazor, *The Makhteshim Country: A Laboratory of Nature.* "Prologue," pg1.

The problem with the camels is two archaeologists from Tel Aviv University, Erez Ben-Yosef and Lidar Sapir-Hen, stated that according to their research, camels were not domesticated in Canaan (Israel) until 900 BC. Their findings prompted *National Geographic* to claim, "While there are conflicting theories about when the Bible was composed, the recent research suggests it was written much later than the events it describes."[4] If true, this destroys the Bible's credibility.

There are even scholars who balk at the idea of Pharaoh giving camels to Abraham, since the text doesn't seem to link Pharaoh with what Abraham owned, only that he treated Abraham well for Sarah's sake. "The princes also of Pharaoh saw her, and commended her before Pharaoh: and the woman was taken into Pharaoh's house. And he entreated Abram well for her sake: and he had sheep, and oxen, and he asses, and menservants, and maidservants, and she asses, and camels." (Genesis 12:15-16)

The word *yâtab* (yuhTAV) is used twice for entreated and well. Its literal meaning is to cause to be sound, beautiful, happy, successful, right. In the over twenty meanings *Strong's Concordance* gives for *yâtab*, [be accepted, amend, use aright, benefit, be (make) better, give, etc.] the sense that Pharaoh wanted to make it right between Abraham and himself seems clear. How he did this we assume was through Abraham receiving something, like all those animals and servants from... someone.

The camel issue has caused scholars, including Bible scholars, to believe the account of Abraham was either written much later, like *National Geographic* quickly claimed, during the First Millennium BC or embellished later on. Either of these views undermines the historical accuracy of Genesis. We have already proven Abraham represents the

---

[4]Mairav Zonszein, "Domesticated Camels Came to Israel in 930 B.C., Centuries Later Than Bible Says," *National Geographic*, February 10, 2014.

historical setting and culture put forth in the Ebla Tablets and Mari Texts, so what about these camels? Do they prove scribes invented the story or exaggerated it?

Martin Heide compared the biblical text, archaeological inscriptions mentioning camels and zooarchaeological data. Zooarchaeology is the part of archaeology that studies what was left behind when something died like bones, hides, shells, scales, etc. It helps archaeologists know which animals people ate and domesticated and how this diet affected ancient people. After reading Heide's work, the key question to ask when examining the evidence for Abraham and his camels may be "One hump or two?"

Heide concluded from his research that the Bactrian camel, two humped, was domesticated and in use during the Third Millennium BC, possibly before.[5] The two humped camel originated east of the Zagros Mountains near what is today Turkmenistan, Afghanistan and Iran. A handy beast of burden, its popularity and availability spread west toward Harran and south into Iraq.

It is listed in Sumerian and Akkadian inscriptions as an elephant of the road or mountain. Deliveries of camels may have been recorded, if the experts are deciphering shipment lists correctly. Also recorded are references to camel fodder.

A small copper statue of a Bactrian camel with a harness in the Metropolitan Museum of Art in New York City dates to the Second or Third Millennium BC. Also dating to that era are clay figurines of two humped camels pulling carts. A Syrian cylinder depicts a Bactrian camel with riders, and a Sumerian poem mentioned the goddess Inanna asking for camel's milk. The poem lends an extra biblical source to

---

[5] Heide, Martin, "The Domestication of the Camel: Biological, Archaeological and Inscriptional Evidence from Mesopotamia, Egypt, Israel and Arabia, and Literary Evidence from the Hebrew Bible ," Ugarit Forschungen, 42, 2011, 148-184.

Genesis 32:15 where Jacob gave Esau thirty milk camels.

According to the San Diego Zoo website, camels are adults when they are seven years old. They carry their young for twelve to fourteen months, and the calves nurse ten to eighteen months. By this we can see what an investment Jacob had in giving away thirty milk camels and their young.

Have you ever tried to milk a wild goat? Catching one is hard enough. Andrew Ucles tried it in Australia and seriously injured himself. A camel is bigger than a goat. If camels were milked, they were most likely domesticated.

The dromedary, one hump, was widely domesticated after the Bactrian camel, just as Erez Ben-Yosef and Lidar Sapir-Hen observed. But the dromedary was in use in southern Arabia and Egypt before it was common in Canaan. References in Sumerian inscriptions call this camel the donkey of the sea. Near Aswan Egypt is a carving showing a man leading a dromedary by a rope. It dates to the Sixth Dynasty, the time some scholars think Abraham visited Egypt.

But there is more evidence. Dating to the First Dynasty is a small jar in the shape of a camel carrying a basket. A tablet showing men riding and leading camels dates even earlier. Clearly, Abraham could have had either one humped camels or two. It just depends where he got them.

If he had any, you would think there would be some evidence of camels in Canaan dating to his lifetime. There is. Camel bones have been found near Arad and Jericho.[6]

Heide points out that Abraham is said to have camels, but his son Isaac is not. We cannot eliminate the possibility, however. It is true he did not travel as much as Abraham did. But, Isaac was certainly rich enough to buy one if he wanted. His son Jacob traveled back to Harran

---

[6]T. M. Kennedy, "The Date of Camel Domestication in the Ancient Near East." AFBR

and is said to own camels in Genesis 30-32. These verses in Genesis reveal where Jacob's camels originated, northern Mesopotamia, and perhaps what type they were, two humped.

To say, "There are too many camels in the Bible, out of time and out of place," as *The New York Times* published,[7] and, "Camels probably had little or no role in the lives of such early Jewish patriarchs as Abraham, Jacob and Joseph..." is to ignore a lot of convincing evidence. So Christians, let's not and use the information made available to us.

Another issue with Abraham's possessions in Genesis 12:16 is the order in which they are listed. Scholars note that it is unusual for the servants to be listed in between donkeys. Was this evidence of the low position of servants, as if they were animals? Or, were these inserted at a later date to impress us and exaggerate Abraham's wealth? Perhaps they are only symbolic of this wealth?

Actually the peculiar order of the possessions is to highlight their value. The most common livestock to own was sheep and goats. Cattle were a step up and so were male donkeys. But if you were to have male donkeys it would be even better if you could own female donkeys and thus be able to raise purebreds to sell.

Concerning servants, which were more common than camels due to poverty and war, it would be wonderful if they could marry and become loyal members in your household. Camels are named last because they were the most exotic and valuable. The order is to show the extent of Abraham's wealth. Genesis 13:2 tells us he had a lot of cattle. His silver and gold, if Pharaoh didn't give him any, was at this time a product of his livestock dealings perhaps.

---

[7]John Noble Wilford, "Camels Had No Business in Genesis," *The New York Times,* Feb. 10, 2014.

We do not know for sure how long Abraham was in Egypt before his episode with Pharaoh began. We do not know how long Sarah was in Pharaoh's house or how long it took before Pharaoh realized Sarah was the only one without the plague. We do not even know if it was God's idea for Abraham to travel to Egypt. Most likely, it was not.

Later, God gave Abraham a dark vision of his descendants' bondage. It must have touched him deeply and reminded him of his experience in Egypt. Abraham was adamant that his son Isaac not leave Canaan. So was God. The closest Abraham ever went to Egypt again was Gerar, but that resulted in the Abimelech incident.

We also have no indication God talked to Abraham in Egypt. It could have been Abraham was experiencing a drought of another kind. He had allowed fear to dictate in the matter of the famine and Sarah's beauty. He realized there was no one in those places he went that feared God, so he became afraid of them.

This reveals the evil character the false gods produced in their Canaanite and Egyptian worshippers. We need to understand it was a real threat; Abraham didn't imagine the danger. He did what he could to protect himself and even Sarah. But it wasn't enough. He needed God.

He also wasn't convinced he was going to be blessed in Canaan during a famine. He decided to leave the place God had given him to seek his own provision. The result was a disaster. But God turned it into a teachable moment, and Abraham never left Canaan again.

The Bible warns the fear of man is a snare, but anyone who trusts God will be safe. (Proverbs 29:25) God did not give Abraham a spirit of fear. Abraham allowed himself to look at his situation and think on it to the point that it was more true than God's blessing. Eventually his fear brought to him what he dreaded. Fear is a type of faith, faith that whatever you fear is going to happen. It becomes pictures in your mind and words you speak to yourself and others. Abraham would come to know these things. We know because his life teaches us.

When Abraham left Egypt he had a destination in mind. He returned to Bethel and Ai where he had established his camp, the place where he had built an altar. But it doesn't seem as if the altar was still standing. The Bible says he returned to the place not the altar.

Abraham worshipped the Lord anyway. This time he had more than a safe trip to be thankful for. This time he knew a bit more about the God he was trusting in. His servants had witnessed God's goodness to them, and the new servants were privy to their master's devotion to a God who bore no image carved in wood, clay or stone.

Lot was still traveling with Abraham. By this time he was old enough to be on his own. Scholars puzzle over who Lot may have married. Some think it may have been Iscah. Poor Iscah. Experts struggle to fit her into the story somewhere. For this study, let's just agree with the rabbis for now and say she is Sarah.

God was blessing Abraham and that blessing was spilling over into the lives of those who were with him, including Lot. After they returned to their home in the hill country between Bethel and Ai, they soon discovered they had another problem. This time it wasn't a drought; it was abundance.

Both men had too much stuff in an area where there were other herdsmen. When Abraham had first arrived in Shechem, the Bible told us there were already people there. Abraham and Lot were trying to stay out of their way.

Not all of Canaan's children listed in Genesis 10:15-18 lived in what you may think of as Canaan. Many textbooks refer to the Phoenicians as the biblical Canaanites and indicate a thin strip along the Mediterranean

Sea as their home. Phoenician is the Greek word for Canaan and was later used in history to replace the Semitic term. Canaan, however, was used at Mari, Nuzi and was found in the Hurrian language.

Babylon was still using the word Canaan in 1100 BC and Egypt in 900 BC. St. Augustine claims Punic (Phoenician) peasants called themselves Chanani. The Phoenicians were pressed into the coastland, however, after Joshua and King David's time. Then, they were attacked by the arrival of the Greeks under Alexander the Great.

But Canaan's children were a mix of tribes, not just the Phoenicians. They ranged from northern Syria, south to the border of Egypt and east of the Jordan River. Their territorial boundaries are listed in Genesis 10:19.

History shows the movement of Canaan's children as they moved out from around Ararat into southern Turkey, down into Syria and eventually into the Promised Land. The last to arrive in large numbers may have been the Amorites. But there were already representatives of these people living there when Abraham arrived.

Those living in modern day Lebanon were Sidon, Canaan's oldest son and his family. His name was also the name of a city. This was the pattern— man, family, town. Here are the territories of more Canaanites: the Arkites, the city of Arka (Tell Arka) is northeast of Tripoli, King David had a friend, Hushai, who was an Arkite; the Arvadite, also a city, Arvad; the Sinite, northern Lebanon, cities of Sinum, Sinna and Syn.

The Zemarkites lived in Syria. Tell Kazel is their ancient city of Sumer. The Amorites were also in Syria. The Hamathites' territory lay near the foot of Mt. Hermon in the Golan Heights and western Syria and northern Lebanon. The Girgashites lived near the Sea of Galilee.

The Hivites and the Jebusites were located in the central region of Canaan near Shechem and Jerusalem respectively. The Hivites were the Gibeonites who fooled Joshua. We learned earlier that the Hivites and Jebusites tribes may have also been part of the Hurrian people in northern Mesopotamia. Some of the Canaanites were very tall in this central region. The Israelites called them giants. Abraham doesn't mention any giants by name.

Bryant G. Wood informs us that the Hethites get confused with the Hittites (Hatti)[8], a northern people who lived in Turkey and were related to Noah's son Japheth. The Hittites established a major empire, but were not living in Canaan when Abraham was. The Hethites were living there, in the hill country around Hebron and Jerusalem. Hebron was one area where the giants lived.

The Perizzites are listed as living in Canaan, but they are not named in Genesis 10. Their name describes a rural people living in unwalled towns. They were among the people Israel could not eliminate completely. Perizzite may be a word like habiru, referring to a mix or classification of people. Perhaps they were hardy, rural farmers.

The Perizzites and Canaanites were living with Abraham and Lot in the area of Bethel and Ai when they started having problems. Cattle need pasture and water, but Abraham and Lot had too many cattle for the land to sustain them all. Something needed to change.

Abraham probably sold his sheep and goats and cattle and donkeys at the stock market centers in the cities. Anyone who is familiar with raising livestock on a larger scale knows the point is to provide for yourself and to sell at a profit. But feed lots like those in Nebraska and eastern Colorado were not a thing in ancient Canaan.

Near Ur in southern Iraq there were towns set up to hold animals for slaughter, for sacrifice and consumption. It seems the traders

---

[8] Bryant G. Wood, "Hittites and Hethites: A Proposed Solution to an Etymological Conundrum." AFBR

contacted their suppliers and traders brought animals to market. The system operated much like the ranchers, beef buyers and stock yards of today. There may have been a few cattle drives or sheep and goat drives, but Abraham had servants to do that if he wanted.

The nomadic ranchers in Canaan were more sedentary than traveling merchants. Sedentary, meaning staying in a spot to watch over their stock and moving to new grazing ground when necessary. The closest modern equivalent may be the Yörüks and Yomuts living in the Taurus Mountains. Of course, you have to overlook their cell phones, trucks, jeans and t-shirts.

There are still Bedouins in Israel's Negev region, but they are Arabic and increasingly motivated by Islamic terrorists groups. Their loyalty to tribe and clan has shifted in recent years to Allah and anti-Semitism. With their populations doubling every year, the Negev Bedouin has become a security concern for Israeli citizens.

We have already learned the habiru and Amorite nomads were sometimes considered a threat to nearby cities in ancient Mesopotamia. While Abraham had no plans to upset local governments like the Bedouin or Amorite, his presence was felt among the Canaanites and Perizzites around Bethel and Ai.

One reason scholars believe Abraham was a traveling merchant is because they cannot understand his wealth being earned any other way. But God already stated how wealth would come to him. In Genesis 12:2 God told Abraham to go out from his father's home and people to a land that He would show him. He stated multiple things He would do for Abraham.

One of the strongest statements a person can make in English is I will to show their intent to do something. I will try to do is a weaker statement. I want to do is also limp. Both of these are more uncertain because they imply a lack of ability. I will carries the sense that you possess the power to see that "it" gets accomplished.

In Genesis 12:2 we witness God declaring a preferable outcome, deciding its course and determining His intent. He was agreeing to benefit Abraham in various ways. God's strong desire was to make Abraham a great nation and to make his name great. His intent was to bless him. Bless is *barak*. In this word is a wonderful picture of our good God. It means to kneel in respect, to give a valuable present to congratulate. This is what God was doing for Abraham. He was honoring him by offering him something valuable.

Deuteronomy 28:1-14 is a list of these valuable things. It is a picture of abundant wealth, health and deliverance. This is what was contained in the word bless for Abraham. And because God is a generous God, He commanded that anyone who treated Abraham well would receive benefits too. This is why we see Lot prosperous and Abraham's servants sticking with him.

On the other hand, if you treated Abraham with contempt, if you wished him harm or cheated him, you could expect the direct opposite of abundant wealth, health and deliverance. The list of curses beginning in Deuteronomy 28:16 spells it out if you have trouble imagining what types of things this might include. This was why Pharaoh ended up with a plague, why Abimelech was threatened with death.

Modern Christians hesitate at God's extravagant promises contained in His blessing. But it extends to those who follow Jesus and have taken Him as their Lord. There are references in the New Testament that state this. Paul wrote through the inspiration of the Holy Spirit in Galatians 3:13-14,29:

> Christ hath redeemed us from the curse of the law,
> being made a curse for us: for it is written, Cursed is

every one that hangeth on a tree: That the blessing of Abraham might come on the Gentiles through Jesus Christ; that we might receive the promise of the Spirit through faith... And if ye be Christ's, then are ye Abraham's seed, and heirs according to the promise.

This is God's intent. He has already accomplished the path for it to be realized, and that path is obedience to His word. As Christians, all we need to do is receive Jesus and trust Him.

Abraham had to set out from Harran. He had to walk the land as God told him and begin proclaiming God's name in that place. He did, and God gave him the power to get wealth as it says in Deuteronomy 8:18. The blessing passed to Isaac who became so powerful the Philistine king in Gerar told him to move away. He feared Isaac was becoming more powerful than he was.

Isaac's son Jacob understood the power of the blessing. God told Jacob's mother, Rebekah, that Jacob was going to inherit the blessing, so when Isaac made plans to ignore God's choice and bless Esau instead, she made sure Jacob got it. Jacob revered the privilege of birthright and God's provision. He built his future from them.

When Abraham was in Canaan there were other successful herdsmen. When Isaac was in Gerar and the Negev there were other prominent nomads. When Jacob went back to his uncle Laban near Harran, Laban realized there was a supernatural favor bestowed on Jacob. What other wealthy men saw in the patriarchs went beyond luck and hard work.

The Israelite men's prosperity was lasting, and it didn't cost them anything. It was God's blessing that caused Abraham's flocks and herds to thrive, to be chosen above others to be bought.

Abraham lifestyle resembled his Amorite and Canaanite neighbors. He lived outside of the towns, his encampment was large and prosperous, he could rent or purchase land for his needs, farming or grazing, and he was gaining respect in the local population. And, envy.

His herdsman and Lot's herdsman started arguing with each other. The cattle were mixing, trespassing. The livestock was hungry and thirsty. It got crowded and stressful.

"And there was a strife between the herdmen of Abram's cattle and the herdmen of Lot's cattle." (Genesis 13:7) It got uncomfortable for Abraham because James 3:16 says, "...where envying and strife is, there is confusion and every evil work."

Abraham did not want their need for land to disrupt the local herders. The strife between two families was enough. Abraham did the wise thing. James 3:17 goes on to say, "But the wisdom that is from above is first pure, then peaceable, gentle, and easy to be intreated, full of mercy and good fruits, without partiality." Abraham decided to make peace with Lot.

Lot either had no solution or was respectively waiting for Abraham to move. Perhaps Lot was content with sulking. Abraham's offer to his nephew was a generous one. Even though Abraham told him it was time to separate and to go out on his own, he allowed Lot first pick of the land in any direction he chose. It was a gentle response full of mercy. It also shows Abraham learned his lesson: God could bless him no matter what the weather or the land.

Lot chose the best for himself. He picked east, the area near the Jordan River because it was well watered. It is the first time we see Lot thinking or doing anything. His choice seems selfish to us perhaps, but Abraham was graciously offering Lot a gift. And he was going to need it because Lot wasn't a hundred percent obedient.

After Lot had packed up his tents, his herds and servants, Abraham may have looked around and wondered what he was going to do. The land was used up perhaps. He may have felt alone. There was something unsettling about watching Lot walk away with his possessions in tow.

He had been obedient to what God wanted him to do. He may have reminded himself God promised to bless him. It just looked hard at the moment.

It was then God spoke to him again. A greater promise than before. He told him:

> Lift up now thine eyes, and look from the place where thou art northward, and southward, and eastward, and westward: For all the land which thou seest, to thee will I give it, and to thy seed for ever. And I will make thy seed as the dust of the earth: so that if a man can number the dust of the earth, then shall thy seed also be numbered. Arise, walk through the land in the length of it and in the breadth of it; for I will give it unto thee. (Genesis 13:14-17)

Lift up thine eyes, God said. Abraham did not have to worry. In this message, God was more detailed in what He wanted to give Abraham. But this time God added something. Was it a condition? It seemed it depended on Abraham. All the land he could see. What did it mean?

The Egypt Incident

*A*braham *sat under the tree shading his tent. The sun was about to sink behind the western hills. Dirt covered his feet and hands. It had been a long day of separating out cattle, sheep and goats. Still the dust hung over the wadi below, like a thin veil in the fading light and stifling heat.*

Sarah had gone up the mountain hoping to see a last glimpse of Lot's family. His young daughters had been a comfort to her. Now they were gone.

He swallowed, his throat dry, parched by the dust and searing sun. He and Sarah were alone now. No family. Abraham pushed the fear down. There was always Eliezer... Abraham stared into the sliver of turquoise blue painted above the mountains.

He scooped a handful of white dust from the stones littering the path. He chuckled as he looked at it. Could it be true? Had Yhôvâh spoken to him again? The answer settled in his heart. Yes, it was the voice of Yhôvâh.

He stood, letting the sand fall through his fingers. Looking out over the horizon he squinted as far as he could see. Yes, he smiled. I see it. North. He turned. South. He smiled. East. He chuckled. West.

"I see it," he whispered.

He walked in a circle his eyes fixed on the farthest reaches of land surrounding him.

"I see it!" he shouted.

He imagined great flocks covering the hills. His. Cattle and donkeys coursed along the wadis. His. He could live anywhere. Graze his herds anywhere. It was all...his.

"I see it, Yhôvâh!"

The breeze passed over the ridge whipping his robe against his legs. He began to laugh. In the morning, he too would gather his men, flocks, herds and tents. It was time to see what else this land of promises offered him.

Chapter 5
The Not So Legendary Battle of Siddim

Bethel was located in what many refer to as the biblical heartland of Israel. It is the second most mentioned city in the Bible after Jerusalem. Today the site of ancient Bethel is El Bireh in the West Bank.

Beth-El was the place where God spoke to His people. Its original name had been Luz, but Jacob renamed it Beth-El, House of God, because there he saw angels going back and forth from heaven to earth. He returned to Bethel after his sons had attacked Shechem. He was afraid the Canaanites would plot revenge, and God led him back to the place of angels.

Joshua had brought the Israelites back to this region before he died, and people continued to return to seek God there during the time of the Judges. The Ark of the Covenant was kept in Bethel for a while. Deborah judged there, and Samuel visited there as part of his ministry to Israel.

But Bethel's prestige as God's house came to an end under Jeroboam. He had a golden calf made and set it up in Bethel for the Israelites of the Northern Kingdom. He said, "... behold thy gods, O Israel, which brought thee up out of the land of Egypt." (1Kings 12:28-29)

It became a house of idols as the prophet Hosea called it, and Jeremiah and Amos used it as an object lesson. The place Abraham and his family had honored was corrupted, polluted and eventually forgotten. Bethel is not even mentioned in the New Testament.

It is said of God that He is no respecter of persons. He requires obedience from all; that is His standard. It is up to man if he chooses to uphold His standard or not. Abraham upheld God's standards the best he knew how. It was not his goal to rebel against the God who brought him into Canaan. When God told him to move from the area of Bethel and walk the land, he immediately went north toward Hebron.

Hebron (khevRONE) means association. It is an ancient city, but it was not sitting at the site of our modern Hebron. Today's city spreads below Abraham's, surrounding the Cave of the Patriarchs. At the time of Abraham it was fields. Abraham's Hebron is Tel Hebron near Jebel Rumeida which overlooks the modern city. It has a spring, and olive trees and a type of wild mustard grow there.

In Abraham's day Hebron was the most important city in the Judean hills, and it still is. Kirjatharba is another name for Hebron according to Genesis 23:2, and so is Mamre, Genesis 13:18. Some scholars believe this shows that the city was large enough to be divided into sections or quarters.

In 1999 archaeologist Emanuel Eisenberg discovered that the Early Bronze Age Hebron had been fortified with a wall, twenty feet thick. Large irregular rocks piled fourteen feet high, leveled with mud brick, may have originally stood over twenty feet high.

But archaeology in the West Bank can be dangerous. In 1956 four archaeologists touring Israel were killed at Ramat Rachel by Jordanian soldiers from across the border. Archaeological work in Hebron stirs conflict with Palestinians who want to claim Hebron as part of an independent Palestinian state. For ten years work stopped. By 2014, 2,000 Israeli soldiers were stationed there to protect the 700 Jewish residents, and archaeologists continued their excavations.

Discoveries have included Jewish baths called *mikvaot* as well as King David's pool. Some wonder if the site of the pool was near David's first palace. There are several Hebrew tombs in Hebron: Othniel Ben Kenaz, Israel's first judge; Ruth; King David's father, Jesse; Abner, King Saul's general; the Cave of the Patriarchs.

There are other exciting finds such as a wall archaeologists date to the time of Noah. They found 4,000 year old stairs which led up to the city gates where Abraham purchased his cave tomb. They discovered an Israeli four-room house and pottery inscribed with the Hebrew word *Hevron* on them. Other finds included seals dating to Hezekiah on jars used for the army fighting Sennacherib perhaps, and black stains on pillars which show fire damage, probably when Sennacherib attacked the city.

Hebron, like Shechem and Bethel, was an important site in the Old Testament. Hethites lived there, the sons of Heth and descendents of Canaan. It was the only place where Abraham bought ground, the place where Caleb carved out a territory for the tribe of Judah, the place David chose for his first capital.

But before Caleb and David, Abraham chose Hebron as his home. He wandered over to pastures in Beersheba for the winter and spring and returned to Hebron for the summer and fall. Its city was old, even when he saw it.

White limestone boulders, settled and stacked, created its high wall around the city. It must have been impressive. Some scholars think people made up the story about giants living there because Hebron's walls were so high and the stones so big only a giant could have built it.

Abraham came to Hebron from the south. He saw its walls. He

walked its ancient steps. Trees grew out of hills where rock outcroppings gleamed in the sun. Gentle breezes rustled the buff colored grasses and blue skies stretched across the valleys and wadis below. But Abraham never described the city. He only mentioned it had a gate.

Some Bibles say Abraham came to the plain of Mamre (mamRAE) while others say the oaks of Mamre. We learned the Hebrew word *'ēlôn* means strong tree or oak. A long time after Abraham had died, people began making up legends and honoring a tree they said was the tree of Abraham. Dr. Shaul Bar thinks Aramaic translators substituted the word plain because they wanted to separate Abraham from pagan tree cults and from believers honoring what they considered sacred trees.[1]

But the Bible tells us this was not one tree like the one at Moreh. The tree at Moreh was probably a landmark. At Hebron, Abraham set up his tents under a grove of trees which provided shade during the summer. Mamre is known to be the name of a man, a friend of Abraham. Dr. Bar states the area was most likely named for the family. Supporting his theory is a river named after Mamre's brother Eshcol. Dr. Bar thinks Abraham lived in that general neighborhood or quarter, outside the city wall, of course.

Abraham bonded with three men of this city, Mamre, Eshcol and Aner, through an agreement of sworn loyalty. We call such an agreement a covenant. We'll talk about covenants later, but for now let's understand they made a pact of friendship that made them brothers forever.

Again Abraham built an altar after he arrived. His loyalty to God did not waver even though he dwelt near to this important city in the vicinity of Amorite nomads and their gods. His separation from Lot had been according to God's plan. Lot did not have a share in Abra-

---

[1] Dr. Shaul Bar, "Abraham's Trees" *Irish Biblical Studies* Vol 28, Issue 1 pg10.

ham's promise. He had been privileged to begin his household and gain wealth along with his uncle, but now his life was his responsibility, governed by his choices. Those choices were about to get him in serious trouble.

Lot had moved east of the Jordan River because he saw the area was well watered. Archaeologist Gary Byers says in his article,[2] "The Jordan River Valley, The Jordan River and The Jungle of the Jordan," that the remains of elephants, hippopotami and alligators are found at sites in Israel, predating the earliest sites in Africa.[3] This lets us know the region had a lot more water than it does today. The Jordan River was wider and deeper in ancient times.

During the Early Dynastic Period of Mesopotamia when Lot lived in the southern Jordan Valley, an Elamite king named Chedorlaomer ruled over at least five cities in Canaan. He made them pay a tax to him. The cities paid the tax for twelve years and in the thirteenth year they rebelled. In the fourteenth, Chedorlaomer gathered three kings, vassals or allies, and came from what is today Iran to fight the rebellious kings in Canaan.

This account of the nine kings listed in Genesis 14 has generated skepticism even among believers. If you search the internet in regard to Genesis 14, the majority of sites chews the same tidbits of error and spits out the same opinion: there is absolutely no evidence for this account anywhere. It is thought the story was inserted into Jewish his-

---

[2] Gary Byers, "The Jordan River Valley, the Jordan River and the Jungle of the Jordan," Associates for Biblical Research, June 6, 2007.

[3] "The researchers had reported last year that they had found evidence of modern man - homo sapiens - in a tunnel at Kafr Qasem dating back 400,000 years, at least 200,000 years earlier than when he was found in Africa, but they had no explanation for this... These new findings would indicate that modern man developed in this region earlier than in Africa, and undermines the widely held belief that man developed in Africa and from there wandered to other continents." Zafrir Rinat, "Disappearance of Elephants in Land of Israel May Have Led to Birth of Modern Man," *Haartz*, Dec 13, 2011.

tory by Jews living in Babylon— just like other cultures embellished their history with fanciful literature. We cannot accept that conclusion, however. The Bible has been proven to be historically, geologically, geographically and anthropologically accurate.

Nevertheless, supposedly you will discover 1) there are no kings of the Middle Bronze Period named anything close to Chedorlaomer 2) nothing is known about the other kings so it is decided they did not exist and 3) many claim, since there is no evidence, the account is made up, as if every speck of historical data has been uncovered, deciphered and filed away.

Others are convinced, even if the kings prove at some point to be real historical figures, the Bible writers inserted the story into Genesis when they were captives in Babylon to make Abraham look important. The basic principle of this theory— the Bible is made up by people who were not eyewitnesses— has been proven wrong so many times you would think it could be abandoned by now.

The fact is, there is evidence of Elamite kings with similar names resembling Chedorlaomer. It is true not much is known about early Elamite history. But, Linear Elamite script, one of their earliest writings, hasn't been deciphered yet. And, new discoveries have put Abraham in the Early Bronze I/Early Dynastic period. Taking that into consideration, it seems premature to proclaim the account in Genesis 14 a myth.

On the contrary, what we do know is intriguing. Sumerian inscriptions tell us there were Elamite kings who attacked Sumerian cities such as Lagash and Kish during the Early Dynastic period. The Sumerian King List states one of the earliest documented kings, King Enmebaragesi of Kish, defeated the Elamites.

Settlement at the Elamite capital of Susa dates to the time of Noah after the flood. Susa is one of the oldest cities in Iran and was an important city for ancient Elamites. It served as the capital even during the time historians call it proto-Elamite, meaning original or primitive. Susa became rich as Elamite kings sacked other cities and brought back their goods.

Twelve kings are listed on a king list found at Susa, but the first one, thought to be reigning at the same time as the first dynasty in Uruk, is not named, and scholars know little about them. According to an updated chronology, the kings listed after Sargon of Akkad are considered too late to have lived during Abraham's battle in Genesis 14.

It was first thought that no king would travel from Iran as far as Canaan to wage wars. The tablets at Ebla and Mari, however, have proven otherwise. We now understand they did. Even in the *Epic of Gilgamesh*, Gilgamesh, now known to have been a real Sumerian king[4], was said to have traveled from Iraq to Lebanon.

Theophilus Goldridge Pinches was a British man with a really long name which is why most refer to him as T.G. Pinches. He became an Assyriologist with the British Museum in 1878. An Assyriologist studies the languages, history and archaeology of the whole Mesopotamian region not just Assyria, which is a bit confusing since an Egyptologist studies…Egypt.

Pinches came to the British Museum two years after George Smith, the man who translated the *Epic of Gilgamesh*, had died. Pinches is famous for correcting the spelling and pronunciation of Gilgamesh's name, the original being very different. He is also known for translating two Babylonian texts containing the names Tudhula, Eri-Ekua and Kudur-lachgumal. Since his translation of the name Gilgamesh has stood up to scrutiny and time, his translation of these three names should be respected.

But it isn't; and it wasn't. Skeptics claimed the names might be

---

[4]See *Noah* Flying Eagle Publications

similar to the names in Genesis 14, but they could not be the same men. Albert T. Clay, the Assistant Professor of Semitic Philology and Archaeology at the University of Pennsylvania, responded to Pinches' critics that it should be impossible to have three kings' names identical to the Bible account and not be the same three men in Genesis 14.[5] Modern archaeology has proven they most likely lived at the same time and in the right places.

Early on Professor Eberhard Schrader (1833-1908) thought Amraphel was the Babylonian King Hammurabi whose name was also spelled Amorapil. But more modern theories placed Hammurabi after Abraham, much later. In light of this, Pinches' translation was cast aside. But Pinches wasn't the man who identified Amraphel with Hammurabi, and other scholars thought Pinches' work should stand with its conclusion: the three names were the same as the names listed in Genesis 14.

The wrong identification of Amraphel with Hammurabi has nothing to do with the Bible account. Abraham knew who Amraphel was. And, scholars do not debate (much) that the three men's names on the tablet are as Pinches translated them. Two major points they disagree on are that the men are kings and that they are the same men in the Bible account.

Pinches' first tablet includes these translations[6]:

the lord of lords, Merodach, in the faithfulness of his heart," aided (probably) his servant to subdue (?) some region, " all of it." Then there is a refer-

---

[5] T. G Pinches. Journal of the Royal Asiatic Society of Great Britain and Ireland, 1907, 738-40.

[6] All translations taken from Theophilus G. Pinches, *The Old Testament In the Light of The Historical Records and Legends of Assyria and Babylonia*, (London:Society For Promoting Christian Knowledge, 1903), 223-232.

ence to (soldiers) whom some ruler " caused A to be slain," and as the name of Dur-sir-ilani son of firi-(E)aku follows, there is every probability that it was he who is referred to in the preceding lines.

"An Elamite (king?)" Something was made, apparently by the same personage, into heaps of ruins, "Kudur-lahmal, his son, pierced his heart with the steel sword of his girdle."

"Tudhula the son of Gazza- ... his son fell upon him with the weapon of his hand."

After this there is a passage where the various kings mentioned seem to be referred to, and it is stated that Merodach, the king of the gods, was angry against them, and they were, to all appearance, made to suffer for what they had done.

Pinches' second tablet translation:

After referring to Babylon, and to the property of that city, " small and great," it is said that the gods (apparently) "in their faithful counsel to Kudur-lahgumal, king of the land of Elam . . . said ' Descend.' The thing which unto them was good (he per- formed, and) he exercised sovereignty in Babylon, the city of Kar-Dunias.

The third tablet contains a story about a battle involving Kudur-lahgumal, Babylon, the gods and Tudhuhla. All the tablets read like fantasy fiction, which is why scholars wouldn't believe the tablets had historical value.

But wait a minute. That is what everyone thought about the *Epic of Gilgamesh*— before Gilgamesh's name was found on the Sumerian

King List. As we said earlier, Gilgamesh is now regarded as a real king. Sargon of Akkad also had legends written about him. Could there be a bias against the fact the names might match names in Genesis 14?

The *Epic of Gilgamesh* has hints of truth embedded in its story. In time we may discover the same for Pinches' three tablets. Pinches has left it to others to decipher who the kings are from his translations, and there have been many guesses. It is remarkable, don't you think, that the four rulers had done something in a war that angered the gods and that one may have died in the battle while the others were murdered by their sons? Sounds like a political scandal.

Interestingly enough, the Sumerian King List shows three Elamite kings from the Awan Dynasty, but their names cannot be read because the stone is damaged and only a few letters are visible for the last king, Ku-ul. Pinches thought the early Elamite name for Chedorlaomer would be Kudur-lagamar, meaning servant of the Babylonian god Lagamar.

This might tell us the notion of Chedorlaomer traveling from Iran may be wrong. He may have been reigning in Babylon, Iraq. His Elamite name honors a Babylonian god. In Genesis 14, he is the leader of the kings, a situation that fits the Early Dynastic period.

The Bible states Amraphel was the king of Shinar and is listed first. Genesis 14:1 begins, "And it came to pass in the days of Amraphel king of Shinar, Arioch king of Ellasar, Chedorlaomer king of Elam, and Tidal king of nations." If Chedorlaomer was the king governing the Canaanite city-states and the kings with him seem to be in his command, why is he not listed first? Was Abraham listing a king with whom he was familiar with, such as one from his homeland?

Shinar lay between the Tigris and Euphrates Rivers. It was a region stretching from the north, near Tel Brak, Syria and nearby regions in

Syria and Turkey, to south in what we know as Sumeria. Recent research by Anne Habermehl and others have shown this area to be a possible location for the original Tower of Babel in the plains of Shinar, an apt description of the site, and it was inhabited from the earliest times.[7]

At the very least, we know this northern Shinar was a place of important cities and trade with government ties to all of Mesopotamia. Important to Abraham, perhaps, Shinar was home.

Some scholars have linked Arioch to Eri-Aku the king of Larsa. Archaeological inscriptions assigned to Eri-Aku state Kudur-mabuk was his father and describe him as the father of the Amurru or Amorites. Pinches translates, "To Nannara, his king, Kudur-mabuk, father of the land of the Amorites, son of Simti-silhak. When Nannara received his prayer he made for Nannara ne-zila-maha for his life and the life of his son Arioch, king of Larsa."[8]

According to Madeleine André Fitzgerald, Kudur-mabuk is an unusual name in cuneiform. It is Elamite. But apparently Kudur-mabuk gave his sons Babylonian names. His daughter's name, however, is Elamite.

So, here is another king with a similar Kudur name, this one with a connection to Eri-Aku, another king. Sir Henry Rawlinson thought this man must have been the Chedorlaomer of Genesis 14.[9] Kudur-mabuk's identity and role in Eri-Aku's life is debated. It seems Eri-Aku relied on his father for military strength and they were involved in a few battles. It also is possible Kudur-mabuk gave his son rule over Larsa. Today most believe Warad-Sin to be another name for Eri-Aku.

Pinches described a story on a badly damaged tablet in which Eri-Aku, who must have died before his father, spoke of a king named

---

[7] Habermehl, "Where in the World Is the Tower of Babel?" *Answers Research Journal.*
[8] Pinches, *The Old Testament*, 219.
[9] Pinches, 222.

Tudchal. The problem with Eri-Aku is he is traditionally dated after Sargon of Akkad and nearer to Hammurabi. This means Eri-Aku ruled after Ebla was destroyed and doesn't match the biblical timeline.

Is Eri-Aku the wrong king? Maybe and maybe not. Remember many of the timelines of archaeology and history are assigned and have been proven to be wrong when new discoveries are made. The problem is timelines haven't been corrected. So much good work has been invested into archaeology that many archaeologists are reluctant to mess with the timeline.

But new discoveries in anthropology and archaeology are changing our ideas of early man and his history and putting civilizations in the realm of even more ancient men. This was not thought possible.

Eri-Aku may be the right king and we don't have a correct timeline for his reign. Or, Eri-Aku is the wrong king identified as Arioch. Another theory links Arioch's name with inscriptions in the Mari Archive to Arriwuk of Nuzi.[10] Perhaps more tablets will be translated and published to give us valuable information about Arioch.

The next king to travel with Chedorlaomer was Tidal king of nations. This specific wording, king of nations, refers to a people who were later called Gentiles. Some scholars notice the similarities between the name Tidal and Tudhaliya, the name of a series of Hittite kings. The problem with this theory is that these specific kings are thought to have lived much later than Abraham.

Another idea is Tidal was a Gutian king named Tadgula. Gutium was a kingdom northeast of Sumer near the Zagros Mountains. Unfortunately little is known about them except their kings are listed on the Sumerian King List, and they did rule over Sumer for a while. If they had

---

[10] Matt McClellan, "Abraham and the Chronology of Ancient Mesopotamia," *Answers Research Journal*, Vol. 5 Oct. 3, 2012, pp. 141–150.

a written language, no tablets have been found yet. The language represented by their names is different from every known ancient language.

Other nations did talk about the Gutians, and what they had to say was not flattering. The Sumerians described them as barbaric ruffians, the same image they gave us of the nomadic groups. In the *Curse of Akkad* they were accused of having no restraint. The Gutians' history has led many scholars to conclude yes, they were a nomadic society but a prominent one. Important to us is they were in existence when Abraham lived.

Archaeology has shown us evidence of kings in ancient history that may describe four of the men in Genesis 14. What we are not so good at is lining up their history. Since the Bible has proven accurate concerning minute details before, we can be confident that Chedorlaomer led his friends in a campaign against cities of Canaan and beyond.

The five city-state kings of Canaan have also been highly disputed. But, thanks to archaeologists like Bryant Wood, the Five Cities of the Plain have some solid discoveries to help us find them. We will discuss the cities later; for now let's take a look at the battle called The Battle of the Valley of Siddim involving all nine kings.

Genesis 14:5-7 says:

> And in the fourteenth year came Chedorlaomer, and the kings that were with him, and smote the Rephaims in Ashteroth Karnaim, and the Zuzims in Ham, and the Emims in Shaveh Kiriathaim, And the Horites in their mount Seir, unto Elparan, which is by the wilderness. And they returned, and came to Enmishpat, which is Kadesh, and smote all the country of the Amalekites, and also the Amorites, that dwelt in Hazezontamar.

We've already discussed the four rulers and said they were headed to Canaan because kings there had rebelled against Chedorlaomer's rule. The first city they attacked was Ashteroth Karnaim. Many scholars put this city south of Damascus in the Bashan area of Syria and the Golan Heights in Israel. The ancient kings then followed a course attacking the Zuzims whom the *International Standard Bible Encyclopedia* informs us are related to the Zamzummim and not Dr. Seuss.

The kings proceed southward to attack Shaveh Kiriathaim. These cities are all located east of the Jordan River in the vicinity of the King's Highway. All of them are said to be inhabited by the Rephaim or as in Shaveh Kiriathaim like the Anakim, very tall people called giants, according to Deuteronomy 2 and 3:11. Traveling south still, they attacked the Horite people living near Mt.Seir in ancient Edom or today southern Jordan.

They went south all the way to the Desert of Paran near western Saudi Arabia. It was the end of the road so to speak, and the kings turned to attack Kadesh. Ancient historians Josephus and Eusebius locate Kadesh Barnea in the desert reaching to Petra, Jordan. Modern scholars place Kadesh in the Sinai Peninsula bordering Canaan. Some believe there are two locations with the same name.[11] After Kadesh or En-Mishpat, the kings went to En Gedi (near the Dead Sea) as 2Chronicles 20:2 calls Hazezontamar.

The result was a clean sweep of victories in lands belonging to the Rephaim, the Amalakites and Amorites. News was carried to the five kings living east of En Gedi in Zoar, Zeboiim, Admah, Gomorrah and Sodom. The message was urgent: Chedorlaomer had circled back and was heading for the road close by; expect an attack. The five kings rallied and joined forces in hopes of defeating Chedorlaomer's allied forces.

---

[11]You can read more about the Kadesh Barnea debate in *Moses* by Flying Eagle Publications.

But they were the losers. Running for their lives, many fell into the slime pits uncovered by the receding Dead Sea. Survivors escaped to the mountains. Chedorlaomer and his troops sacked the cities and carried off all the people and plunder they could manage.

A campaign of this scale should have some evidence in the archaeological record. It does. But as usual, it is buried in a mistaken timeline and its mistaken theories.

Torah scholar, Dr. David Ben-Gad HaCohen has studied the periods in history and geology to determine the approximate date this battle might have happened. The Dead Sea during wet periods flooded the southern basin. In dry periods it receded, revealing slime pits. Today the Dead Sea is shrinking and there are even sinkholes almost seven miles deep!

Dr. HaCohen's research states the valley was flooded during the Third Millennium, causing the cities to be built on the south eastern shore. By the late Third Millennium, the Early Bronze age, it was dry. It was also during this period that the cities were destroyed and never occupied again.

Dr. HaCohen sees his research as proving the story was made up, especially since the verses seem to indicate that at the writing of the account the valley was flooded again. The next time the area flooded was during the Second Millennium, the Middle Bronze period. But the timing fits with a corrected timeline of history, putting Abraham in the Early Bronze age when it was dry and Moses, who documented the account for the Pentateuch, in the Middle Bronze age when it was flooded.

Really interesting is the research by Dr. A. J. M. Osgood. His work settled on En Gedi as the key to unlock the correct era for Genesis 14 and the Battle of Siddim. Excavations at En Gedi have revealed the largest settlement to be in the late Chalcolithic period in the Levant just before Early Bronze Age 1. There was also evidence for settlement there during the Kingdom of Israel and in Roman times, both way too late for Genesis 14. The Chalcolithic age, however, overlaps Abraham in an updated timeline.

The Chalcolithic age is not so much defined by time but the characteristics of a migrating people. It began in the north in Turkey and spread into Mesopotamia, Israel, Eastern Europe, Western Europe and south into the Iberian Peninsula. The people kept sheep, goats, and farmed, hunted and gathered food, lived in mudbrick houses and traded with other people living far away. It is typical of what is called the Ubaid and Uruk Expansions.

In other words these were Noah's descendants moving about the earth after the Tower of Babel. Experts say it is difficult to assign a time period because the characteristics of this lifestyle show up in a lot of places over thousands of years, even when other places are more advanced. They estimate this age lasted from 5500 BC- 2000 BC.

In American history, we witness a similar phenomenon not in thousands of years but hundreds. In the east, say New York City, in 1850 people were living in mansions. Tall buildings towered over paved streets. Immigrants poured into the city to work and attend its public schools and colleges. Police roamed the streets to dispel crime. We can safely conclude New York City would be considered an advanced civilization.

But let's move farther west. Same year. 1850. Michigan, for example. Most residents were farmers. People had been trying to tame the wild peninsula for over thirty years. It remained a frontier state for the next eleven years. Farther west in places like Nebraska, Montana, Wyoming, Colorado, North and South Dakota, lands wouldn't even be called the Nebraska Territory and annexed by the United States until 1854. Trading posts and forts dotted the west while people lived scattered throughout in crude log cabins or hunkered down in dirt houses called dugouts.

Native Americans still inhabited the area, living either nomadic or farming lifestyles depending on their tribe. Raids were not uncommon, by either settlers or Natives. Men came from cities to govern the frontier and serve in its forts. Life was hard and many pioneers gave up and returned to the cities.

What would an archaeologist living thousands of years from now do with all the relics he dug up that we know date to 1850? Would he date them all the same year or assign them different periods to show an evolution for man?

This is the type of settlement we see during what experts label the Early Bronze Age 1 and just before it: city builders living at the same time as pioneers settling new frontiers alongside earlier pioneers.

At En Gedi, there is evidence of early pioneers. Excavations also showed settlement at the same time in the Negev near Beersheba and a shared culture, specifically labeled Ghassul IV. Teleilat Ghassul is an archaeological site in the Jordan Valley about fifty miles northeast of the Dead Sea. This is the site archaeologists use to determine if other sites match the Ghassulian characteristics of the Chalcolithic age. En Gedi and the Negev sites were a match.

At En Gedi another discovery in 1960 revealed a cave. Apparently the ancient residents of En Gedi had quickly stashed valuable articles in the cave, but no one came back to get them. It is called the Cave of Treasures. These settlements disappeared at the same time but no one knows why.

Dr. Osgood states "if you plot those sites on a map and realize they all disappeared at the same time, knowing also of the urgency at En Gedi[12], the only thing in history that might accommodate their disappear-

---

[12] Climate change has been blamed for the reason these cultures disappeared, but would climate change be the reason people hastily stashed their valuables and never returned for them? The experts who site climate change as the cause have to ignore a lot of archaeological evidence to the contrary.

ance [and cave stash] is Chedorlaomer's march over the same territory."[13] This would mean there are no thousand year linear stretches between Ghassul IV, Jemdat Nasr and the Early Dynastic I and Early Bronze Age 1. It puts the cities, Chedorlaomer and Abraham all together. Dr. Osgood dates this to 1870 BC when Abraham was about eighty.

The four allied kings ended the Canaanite rebellion by devastating the culprits, the pithy pioneers of the Trans Jordan and southern Israel. But one lucky survivor fled northeast and wound up on the plain among Mamre, Abraham, Eshcol, and Aner. His bad news became Abraham's bad news when he revealed Lot and his family were among the captives Chedorlaomer took as he left Sodom and headed north.

Another point of contention concerning Genesis 14, is Abraham's campaign against four established kings from important cities and their experienced, well armed troops. But what is the problem? We've already learned by scholarly research how nomadic bands helped kings fight and win battles. In Abraham's case, Genesis 14, we see who had fresher men and a stronger band of nomads.

Genesis 14:14 says Abraham "armed his trained servants, born in his own house, three hundred and eighteen, and pursued them unto Dan."[14] Skeptics read 318 men and scoff at the idea of such a small army routing four kings and their troops. But historically, it's been done before. The Battle of Morgarten in 1315 between Swiss farmers (armed with rocks and staffs fitted with axes) and Leopold I of Austria is one example. The key was strategy and opportunity.

And Abraham had a strategy. Abraham divided his troops into two groups. The verse says they were trained, and since we are reading about a battle we assume they were trained in warfare.

---

[13] A.J.M. Osgood, "Times of Abraham."

[14] Excavations at Tel Dan confirm the existence of a city since 4500 BC.

The word translated trained is *chânîyk* (hkahNEEKH) and means instructed, trained or practiced. What is important is *chânîyk* is used once in the Bible. But it was found in Egyptian Execration Texts[15] dated to the Twelfth Dynasty.[16] This points to a writer living in that era—Moses—and not a writer living when the Israelites were living in Babylon hundreds of years later.

Now back to the battle…There may have been more than 318 men because Mamre, Eshcol and Aner were with Abraham. They could have had trained servants too. Or, that was the total and it doesn't matter because it was enough. Abraham and his men caught up with the kings near the ancient city of Dan south of Mt. Hermon.

A surprise attack at night was successful. Abraham chased the kings all the way to Damascus; out of Canaan is the important fact. "And he brought back all the goods, and also brought again his brother Lot, and his goods, and the women also, and the people." (Genesis 14:16)

News of the victory spread. As Abraham approached the southern regions of Canaan, the King of Sodom came out to greet him. This man may have been the successor of the ruler who "fell" in Genesis 14:10. He came empty handed, but the king (melek) of Jerusalem (Salem) did not. His city had escaped the attack.

"And Melchizedek king of Salem brought forth bread and wine: and he was the priest of the most high God. And he blessed him, and said, Blessed be Abram of the most high God, possessor of heaven and earth: And blessed be the most high God, which hath delivered thine enemies into thy hand." (Genesis 14:18-20)

---

[15] E. Ray Clendenen, "Did Those Places Really Exist?" *Apologetics Study Bible* (Nashville, Tennessee:Holman) 25

[16] Amon Ben-Tor, "Do the Execration Texts Reflect an Accurate Picture of the Contemporary Settlement Map of Palestine?" The Hebrew University, Jerusalem pg 3, huji acedamia.edu

Melchizedek, both king and High Priest of God, offered honor to Abraham, treating him like royalty. He refreshed Abraham's tired men with food and drink, and Abraham gave him an offering from the plunder they brought back. The tithe Abraham offered to the king/priest, and the sacrifices offered on altars from even Cain and Abel show us that the worship practices of the Hebrews had roots reaching all the way back to before the flood.

Ancient worship of God differed from other religions. Simple uncut stone altars were used to worship God. Uncut stones were set up as pillars. These stones were pure as God created them. Channels were cut into the bases of altars to collect blood, but there were no ornately carved constructions like at Göbekli Tepe.

Israeli archaeologist and one of the most respected experts on Jerusalem, Eli Shukron, believes he has found one such altar. Underneath the hills of Jerusalem, he has found evidence of animal sacrifices and olive presses dating back 4,000 years. There are channels cut into rock slab foundations, v's carved out to support tripods for skinning goats and sheep, and hollowed out sections of rock to pass a rope through just high enough to hold a sheep or goat for butchering. It even faces the right way. But his most important find is a simple stone pillar he believes dates to Melchizedek the king and priest of Jerusalem.[17]

To support his idea, Shukron uses Jacob's declaration in Genesis 28:12 and Jacob marking what he thought was the house of God with a stone pillar. Shukron understands that this was a practice among the patriarchs. Likewise, Shukron's stone pillar may be the stone marking Melchizedek's place of worship in Jerusalem. The area was carefully buried. He thinks this occurred during Hezekiah's reign when all wor-

---

[17] Living Passages, *Inside Temple Zero: Eli Shukron talks Melchizedek and the anointing of the House of God.* April 30, 2018. You Tube

ship was to be conducted at the Temple on Mt. Moriah. Hezekiah destroyed pagan sites, but this site was treated with respect. Why?

The possible conclusion? Since the stone sits on bedrock and it is impossible to dig lower, Shukron has discovered Melchizedek's worship site.

Abraham's battle is an important part of his story. It is not just the details of how he rescued Lot and Lot's family. Abraham acted as the leader of the nation, defending its citizens and delivering them when no else could. Canaan was free because of Abraham. Whichever *Kudur* Chedorlaomer was, he was no longer going to fill his treasury with their money. He had been chased out and left with nothing. Perhaps that was the reason for that murderous political scandal we read about.

The King of Sodom just wanted his people back. He made Abraham an offer that seemed generous. "Give me the persons, and take the goods to thyself." (Genesis 14:21) We read Abraham's response and wonder if there is a hint of rebuke in it.

> And Abram said to the king of Sodom, I have lift up mine hand unto the LORD, the most high God, the possessor of heaven and earth, That I will not take from a thread even to a shoelatchet, and that I will not take any thing that is thine, lest thou shouldest say, I have made Abram rich: Save only that which the young men have eaten, and the portion of the men which went with me, Aner, Eshcol, and Mamre; let them take their portion. (Genesis 14:22-24)

Or was Abraham being nice? There is an Ugarit text describing a similar response from King Suppiluliuma to one of the governors of his cities. The governor, Niqmaddu, had sent a message for help against an invading army. He vowed submission as in I-will-never-rebel-against-you-ever-great-king-just-help-me-please. Apparently Niqmaddu's humility was fetching because the Hittite king sent princes and troops.[18] Niqmaddu rewarded the princes after he was delivered, but according to Victor P. Hamilton, concerning himself, the Hittite king replied, "Suppiluliuma, the great king, will not touch anything, be it straw or splinter."[19]

From this example, we see the greater king defending his vassal as his responsibility without compensation. This is the position Abraham took with the king of Sodom. God had given Abraham the land; it was his to defend, and God had enabled him to do it.

Another aspect of Abraham's refusal was he must have been wary of entering into an agreement with an immoral king. Sodom was an immoral place. It had immoral rulers. We know this because the angels did not lead the king out of Sodom before destroying it in Genesis 19. In 2Chronicles 18-20, Jehoshaphat was a good man, but he made alliances with bad men. God wasn't pleased with the friends he made, and Jehoshaphat paid the price for his compromises.

Was Sodom an immoral place in Genesis 14? We might assume so because it wasn't the king of Sodom who was associated with the Most High God in this chapter. But the destruction of Sodom happened over ten years after this battle. The fact remains, Abraham had made a blood covenant with three Amorite men, Mamre, Eshcol and Aner, but he would make no friendship with the king of Sodom. Abraham made it clear to all of Canaan: God was his source, for protection, for victory, for provision. Not one Canaanite could argue with that.

---

[18] Joshua Berman, "Histories Twice Told: Deuteronomy 1—3 and the Hittite Treaty Prologue Tradition." *Journal of Biblical Literature* 132, no. 2 (2013) 234-235.

[19] Victor P. Hamilton, "Abram Meets Two Kings (14:17–24)" *The Book of Genesis: Chapters 1-17* (Grand Rapids:Eerdmans, 1990) 413-414.

*T*all and straight as a Lebanon cedar, Mamre walked up to him leading his camel. "Success has followed you, Abram."

"It follows us, my brother." Abram gestured to Mamre's brothers, their sons and the other Amorites gathering to receive their reward from Sodom's king. His own servants were scattered among them.

Mamre smiled, his lips white against the grime of the desert sands covering his face. They had ridden hard and no one had taken time to refresh themselves. "It is a good thing we have done. Like lions, we have swept this land of jackals."

Abraham stared into the crowd of men as they packed away goods and tucked extra tunics into their belts. He did not want to offend Mamre. But it was Yhôvâh and Yhôvâh only who had given them the victory against proud Chedorlaomer.

"You are the Prince of Hebron." Mamre turned to the men also.

Abram grinned. "Yhôvâh is the Prince I serve."

"Yes." Mamre nodded. "Your God is now the Prince of Hebron and His servant the ruler of men." Mamre almost seemed jealous.

Abram rested his hand on Mamre's shoulder. "I am a shepherd. And a foreign one at that."

Mamre laughed. His shoulders relaxed. He hugged Abraham, kissing the air beside both cheeks and walked into the throng of sweating men.

Abram bowed. Mamre's sons surrounded him and that familiar hollowness crept into Abram's chest. The desire for a son rose inside him like the Jordan overflowing its banks. He tried to push it down, but it only became stronger.

It was a desire that never left him. But it loomed like the mountains south of the Arabah.

"Master." Eliezer trotted to him, his arms laden with raisin cakes. "For you," he said, "to strengthen yourself."

Abram took a slab of pressed raisins. "Keep the rest for yourself." He nodded to the servants. "Speak for them to the king. Make sure they get what is due them."

Eliezer nodded. He was a slight young man and bright, very bright.

Abram coiled his camel's rope. "Return in the morning. I am going ahead now."

Eliezer motioned for the young boy standing by to lead Abram's camel. "Very well, Master. Let Adamu accompany you. He can lead the camel if you tire of walking."

Abram handed the rope to the young servant. He walked in front of the boy, the trees of Mamre in the distance.

"Eat." Abram handed the cake to the boy. Food was not what he wanted. At least Sarai waited for him.

Chapter 6
Making Abraham

Abraham entered Canaan with a promise of inheriting land. As he tentatively began leaning on the promise, he grew in faith and resources. After his successful battle against four kings from Mesopotamia, he had earned a full blown reputation because of his trust in that promise. God's favor upon him was visible and benefited even sinful Canaanites.

But victory's rush didn't linger for Abraham. Something was bothering him. He was thankful God had used him, grateful Lot was safe, encouraged by his friends' and servants' loyalty. But...

There was a sort of unsettledness, a lack of complete joy. On the surface, there may have been shadows, whispers of doubt amongst his neighbors. Were they wise in kicking Chedorlaomer out of Canaan? Would there be another, bigger army coming to retaliate or to take over what Chedorlaomer couldn't hang on to? Time may have grown second thoughts spoken like prophecies from pessimistic lips.

Did any of this affect Abraham? Maybe. Then there was the incident about the reward. The king of Sodom offered Abraham payment for rescuing the villagers. Abraham passed the offer to the men with him, but he did not take a share. The rest of those who went with him were enjoying theirs. Even his servants got stuff for crying out loud. Abraham came home and went back to work. Was he feeling empty? Did seeing Lot renew feelings of loss?

All we really know is time passed, but when God appeared to him next, He appeared in a vision, and His first words were "Fear not, Abram: I am thy shield..." (Genesis 15:1)

Comforting assurance was God's greeting. We know then that Abraham was troubled. Imagine God as your shield. What or who could ever get past Him to do you harm? Abraham had already experienced God as his shield, with the Pharaoh of Egypt and now four other kings.

But God didn't stop there. Abraham may not have received a reward from men, and this may have been by God's direction, but God was his reward. "Fear not, Abram: I am thy shield, and thy exceeding great reward."

Exceeding great. Past great to more than great. Exceeding is *m^eôd* which looks a bit like calculus but is pronounced mehODE. It means with muchness, force, abundance, speedily. We can understand the wow of this great. Speaking of great, it is *râbâh* (ruhVAH), increase, abundance, multiply, nourish, plenty, authority. Put all that together and God was declaring He was Abraham's source of supply for abundant muchness. He was the source of Abraham's authority. You can tack on all those other words too. God was it capital I.

The word for reward is *śâkâr* (suhHAHRDH). The meaning is interesting, since God spoke this of Himself. It is the idea of payment or compensation, a benefit, wages. He was Abraham's wage or compensation for what? For choosing Him. Hundreds of years later, Joshua demanded that the Israelites choose whom they would serve. Abraham had chosen to serve God, and God had rewarded him with His presence, protection and provision.

Some people teach that God told Abraham not to fear because Abraham was afraid of God's presence. It was an awesome event to experience, for sure. Many others fell facedown in the presence of God. Abraham was most likely affected; he just doesn't say how. But God defined Himself as Abraham's shield, in case Abraham was forgetting, because Abraham needed to know. But in this exchange with God, Abraham doesn't seem to be afraid of Him.

Some people also teach that God was speaking of a spiritual reward, as in a heavenly future blessing or just having God's presence was Abraham's reward. Abraham did appreciate God being with him as his offerings prove, but his response shows he clearly understood the words to be a material reward. God had promised Abraham he would become a nation and in a land, a place on earth, He was giving him.

Abraham had already enjoyed material blessings. He was very rich. God was his reward. He had enjoyed safety. God was his shield. Abraham understood all that. He had believed God was with Him. His conviction about those things was the iron rod of resolve that inspired him to chase four kings, like a dog defending its territory, out of Canaan and away from bothering the Canaanites.

Abraham's reply to God seems bold, but at least it tells us what was bothering him. "Lord GOD, what wilt thou give me, seeing I go childless, and the steward of my house is this Eliezer of Damascus? And Abram said, Behold, to me thou hast given no seed: and, lo, one born in my house is mine heir." (Genesis 15:2-3)

Abraham's answer drips with fear. God didn't answer immediately, so Abraham made his case crystal clear. He was accusing God and pointing out what God had not given him, the seed to begin the nation.

He said in essence God's material reward was useless to him because he had no son. Many people believe the same way Abram believed— that it is God who holds back what we desire. We think God does this to teach us something or that it is God only who determines our timetable of receiving what He promised. We think our response to God's promises do not matter and require no action on our part.

But no where do we witness Abram pursuing a child with the same fervor as he did Chedorlaomer. Abram was passively waiting while looking at his childlessness. His frustration was building. But God had already promised a son. Abram was not yet Abraham the father of nations through Isaac because he didn't fully understand God's purpose for his son and didn't realize the thoughts inside him that allowed his childlessness to remain.

He didn't grasp the meaning in God's words to him about being his source of supply. It included having a son. Abraham didn't need to fear failure because God was his shield, enabling him to be triumphant against any type of defeat. If only Abraham could get his eyes off his problem and onto God and stay in that place of trust. Then, he would be pursuing his heir.

Abram, for the first time documented in his own words spoken to God, revealed his heart's desire. All the gold and camels were good for nothing if he had no child because all the wealth would pass to another family. God had promised to give him an inheritance, to make his seed like the particles of sand.

But Abram could not see how it could happen. In fact all he could see was that he had no child. He had married a barren woman. Childlessness greeted him every morning and reminded him every night that his life was passing, his dream dying. It was a situation and a circumstance he could see. It was a repetitive threat of defeat. He saw it and feared.

Abram was struggling. He tried to believe God would give him children. He tried to hang on to the promise God had given him about becoming a great nation and seed (descendants) so numerous they would be like the grains of sand.

But years passed, and it felt like the promise was as light and fleeting as sand falling through his fingers. He needed help, and he wasn't afraid to remind God of His promise. God had given him no seed, neither a son nor a daughter. While his servants had children, while his nephew Lot had children, while his friends had children, Abraham whom God had called went without, and there was nothing he could do about it. He thought.

Some people think faith in God is blind faith, meaning you believe something even though you have no proof, or sight, of it. But God has given us many reasons or proofs to believe in Him. Romans 1:19-20 informs us the created world is clear evidence, so clear that man is without an excuse for refusing to believe in God. Like David, we can know the heavens declare the glory of God. (Psalm 19)

Most of us have more proofs in our lives, or reasons to believe, than just observing creation. Abraham certainly did. Hebrews 11 is called the faith chapter. In it God gives us insight into how faith should behave. "Now faith is the substance of things hoped for, the evidence of things not seen." (Hebrews 11:1) You might think, "Right there the Bible tells us faith isn't seen; it has no proofs!" That is what many people teach, but James says faith without proofs is dead.

Abraham was reminding God of this principle. He knew God had promised him children. Where were they? Finally, he was beginning to act on the promise; he was making a demand on it.

Hebrews 11:1 says faith is substance and evidence. A modern dictionary like *Dictionary.com* may give several definitions for faith, one of which is a belief that is not based on proof. This is the definition many apply to the word faith when it concerns Christianity. It is not the biblical definition, however.

Another definition for faith is a type of collective belief as in a system of religious belief or doctrine, like the Buddhist faith, the Catholic faith, etc. We are not speaking of this definition either. We are discussing a strong conviction, a firm trust in God that He is true and speaks truth.

The word faith is the Greek *pistis*, an assurance, a guarantee, or to be assured of. Substance is *hupostasis* (whoPAHstahsis), to stand by or stand under as to support. Hope is *elpís* (elPEECE), confident expectation or the happy expectation of good. Evidence is *elenchos* (ELaykahs), a proof or proving test by which invisible things are proved.

Let's read the verse with all its meanings: faith is a strong trust in God, a strong trust in His character, in what He said, an assurance that is a guarantee that supports the things you are confidently, happily expecting and puts this principle to a proving test resulting in what you are believing for becoming visible.

That's a mouthful, but it helps us understand how faith is supposed to work. By any rendering of the verse, we can see cracks in Abraham's method of acting it out. We can at least say during this conversation with God, he wasn't confidently expecting a happy outcome.

Hebrews 11:6 says that without faith it is impossible to please God. Abraham was not completely without faith. The verse goes on to say, "for he that cometh to God must believe that he is." Abraham came to God even when his family did not.

But believing there is a God and believing His word is true are two different things in a Christian's life. Abraham knew there was a God. He struggled to receive from the promises in God's word to him. Most Christians find themselves mired in the same place. Abraham didn't fight to believe about prosperity so why children? It was a place he had never seen a hint of hope. His wife had not even so much as miscarried. It was the concept of never that had made a home in his heart.

We may read Abraham's reply to God and cringe at what seems to be disrespect. But God showed no anger. He was attempting to stir Abram's desire so Abraham could receive his son. The whole of Hebrews 11:6 says, "But without faith it is impossible to please him: for he that cometh to God must believe that he is, and that he is a rewarder of them that diligently seek him." To diligently seek God is to search out, investigate, crave and demand (*ekzēteō* eckzayTEHoh)). This is exactly what Abraham did by asking his question.

Someone once said hope is a picture in your head. We think in pictures. If you give a friend the directions to your house, you form images in your head as you speak. If a person tells you about their cat, you picture a cat. Your picture changes as they describe it as a Siamese cat, a kitten or a short-haired tabby.

What you are capable of picturing matters when it concerns receiving from God. Abraham did not see or imagine himself with a child. God had given him dirt to form a picture, but time had passed and the picture faded. God needed to answer Abraham's question and his biggest fear— mainly that Abraham's servant would get everything because God wasn't following through on His promise.

A servant becoming an heir was thought to be part of the myth of Abraham and his story. But the Nuzi adoption tablets and the adoption contracts from Tell Harmal in Baghdad have shown that it was a legal alternative throughout the Ancient Near East. *Tuppi mārūti*, tablets of sonship, were legal documents, carefully kept and accepted before courts as proof of adoption and rights.[1]

---

[1] Dr. Robert Paulissian, "Adoption in Ancient Assyria and Babylonia," *Journal of Assyrian Academic Studies*, Volume 13 No. 2 (1999) pg 9.

Since Abraham had no son, it seems he was planning to adopt Eliezer. In return, Eliezer would take care of Abraham and Sarah in their old age and see that they were buried. Eliezer would then inherit all Abraham had owned.

Most adoptive heirs became secondary heirs if the adoptive couple ended up having a natural born child. A host of stipulations about marriage, inheritance, taking care of elderly parents, etc. could be included in the contract.[2]

Some think Abraham purchased Eliezer when he traveled through Damascus on his way to Canaan. But it was Eliezer's family who had a history working for Abraham or Terah. Abraham says Eliezer was born into his house. How his family came into Abraham's house we don't know, but Damascus enters into their identity somehow.

God corrected Abraham's idea of the servant as his heir. God told him plainly that a child would be born to him. "And, behold, the word of the LORD came unto him, saying, This shall not be thine heir; but he that shall come forth out of thine own bowels shall be thine heir."

The word used for bowels also contains the meaning of uterus. Since God considered a husband and his wife one (the two shall become one), He established that the baby would be born from Abraham's flesh, bowels and uterus. It can also mean heart. This child would be Abraham's heir. Thus, God answered Abraham's complaint and fears.

Still, Abraham needed a new picture. God took him outside and told him to look up. Abraham didn't just need a new picture, he needed a new perspective. This child was going to be given to Abraham through heavenly means. Abraham would later learn how miraculous, but at the moment all he heard was God was doing it.

---

[2] Maria DeJ. Ellis, "An Old Babylonian Adoption Contract from Tell Harmal," *Journal of Cuneiform Studies* 27, no. 3 (1975) pgs 130-51.

God told him to look at the stars and to count them, an impossible task. "And he brought him forth abroad, and said, Look now toward heaven, and tell the stars, if thou be able to number them: and he said unto him, So shall thy seed be." (Genesis 15:5)

This image satisfied Abraham. He believed God's word to him and God counted his trust as righteousness. Righteousness is *tsedâqâh* (tse-dahKAH) meaning right standing, or one who walks a straight path as in Proverbs 4:26-27, "Ponder the path of thy feet, and let all thy ways be established. Turn not to the right hand nor to the left..." English speakers would consider this person morally upright, good or someone with integrity.

But none of those qualities was accomplished by Abraham's effort. Abraham was not righteous on his own. God assigned righteousness to him because Abraham believed God's words and trusted God to do what He said He would do.

God established again the purpose for bringing Abraham from Ur of the Chaldees into Canaan. "And he said unto him, I am the LORD that brought thee out of Ur of the Chaldees, to give thee this land to inherit it." (Genesis 15:7) God was taking the responsibility of fulfilling His word to Abraham upon Himself.

At this point in his conversation with God, Abraham asks another question that may sound like more unbelief. He wanted to know how he would know for sure God was going to give his descendants the land. Maybe you could think of it as Abraham asking for God to make a will Abraham could pass to family.

This is what he wanted, a legal, concrete agreement he could point to as proof of God's pledge. Like the stars, it would help him when his thoughts threatened to dissolve into fear and leave the path of faith. More importantly, it would do the same for his family.

God answered his request by making a blood covenant with him. A covenant in Abraham's day was serious legal business. A word was binding. A blood covenant was unbreakable. Blood covenants were not new, however. Our Mesopotamian archaeological texts attest to that.

In his book, *The Blood Covenant,* Henry Clay Trumbull gives evidence from ancient times of blood covenants in the Middle East, China, Polynesia, North and South America and Africa. The purpose of the covenant was to bind two parties together for their common good. It was a pledge of protection, loyalty, provision and friendship. Since life is found in the blood, the fellowship agreement was for life. If a man broke it, he was killed.

The widespread practice of the ritual and its meaning reveals that it had a common source, as Trumbull and other scholars have noted. According to the Bible, the first blood shed that was specifically mentioned as being shed for the purpose of forming a bond was Abel's sacrifice of a sheep as an offering to God.

You might wonder why a sheep? Because God sacrificed a sheep to clothe Abel's parents, Adam and Eve after they had sinned. It is significant the slain sheep clothed them in their need, a picture of Jesus, the Lamb of God, clothing us in righteousness. The Bible's first depiction of man sacrificing for the purpose of worship shows Abel giving his sheep to God.

Animal sacrifice was also a widespread practice in antiquity. Trumbull writes that to ancient man "Blood is not death, but life. The shedding of blood, Godward, is not the taking of life, but the giving of life. The outflowing of blood toward God was an act of gratitude or of affection, a proof of loving confidence, of inter-union."[3]

Of course not all these gods were God and not all the sacrifices

---

[3] Henry Clay Trumbull. *The Blood Covenant* (New York:Charles Scribner's Sons 1885),pg 148.

were animal. This idea became corrupted as man became evil and perverted worship of the true God. Concerning blood covenants, a second century Roman named Sextus Pompeius Festus wrote that blood mingled with wine and drunk was a type of blood covenant called *assiratum*. *Assir* means blood, and you can see it in this word.[4]

Trumbull tells us *assir* is not a Latin word but can be traced to the Hebrew *asar* meaning to bind together and *issar*. He writes, "Thus we have *asar issar 'al naphesh* to bind a self-devoting vow upon...one's blood."[5] He also points to the Assyrian *esiru*, to bind. *Strong's Concordance* lists *issar* as with a bind or binding obligation. It lists *assar* as used in the giving of a tithe.

That the shedding of blood was binding is an indisputable fact throughout ancient cultures. In Genesis 15:9-18 God directs Abraham to sacrifice a heifer, a goat, a ram, a dove and a pigeon, but not as a burnt sacrifice. Abraham killed them, cut them (except the birds) and arranged them. After dark, a supernatural smoking furnace and a torch passed between the pieces. "In the same day the LORD made a covenant with Abram..." (Genesis 15:18)

Strong's tells us covenant is *berîyth* (bairEETH). It means cutting as in a compact, alliance or treaty made by passing between pieces of flesh. This is the same word used when God made a covenant with Noah. The word and method involved was how we got the term cutting a covenant. Abraham had made this type of agreement with his Amorite friends Mamre, Eshcol and Aner. Now God had made it with him, an unbreakable bond of alliance and provision.

Usually after the men making the covenant had sacrificed the animals and passed between them, they would cook the meat and eat togeth-

---
[4]Trumbull pg 63-65.
[5] Trumbull pg 65.

er. Sometimes God was represented by seven animals or stones in these agreements. Salt was also included in some of the covenants. (Numbers 18:19; 2Chronicles 13:5) Later in history eating and drinking together became the bond, and the pledge was made in an oath to a deity.

Next, God gave Abraham a vision about his descendants becoming captives in a land not their own for four hundred years. Some think it was impossible for Abraham to have known this, and therefore the information must have been inserted by Moses or a later scribe. But biblical prophecy is a fact that cannot be ignored and reasoned away. For Jesus' birth alone, over three hundred prophecies were fulfilled, many referenced in extra biblical sources.[6]

God gave Abraham specific territorial boundaries concerning the land he was to inherit. Since He was making a legal agreement, it was fitting to spell out details of what land was to be owned by Abraham's descendants through the son God gave him. In Genesis 15:19-21 a listing of the occupants of this territory is given. The list changed somewhat by the time four hundred years passed and new groups were listed, but the territory was the same. The boundaries included what is Israel, parts of modern day Syria, Jordan and perhaps northwest Saudi Arabia.

After the encounter ended, it seemed to Abraham things were looking up. He had been given specific details about the future, and God had sealed His promises to him with a covenant. But then time kept passing, empty passing, the same routine. Nothing changed for Abraham even though he stared into the night sky, countless stars encouraging him to hope.

Something changed for Sarah, however. All her life she had known of a common custom available to childless women. She never used it.

---

[6] For more read *Is Jesus God* by Flying Eagle Publications.

It was a common practice included in marriage contracts[7], and even a duty, for a primary wife who was barren to offer a secondary wife to her husband so that he might have an heir. Sometimes a woman would do this for herself. This was Rachel's situation in Genesis 30. While a man could marry another woman, it was up to the wife to offer a concubine. A concubine was like a wife, but had a lower status.

Abraham had never taken a second wife. Sarah had never offered one of her servants to him as a concubine. Obviously, they had made a decision to have a child of their own flesh and blood. They were waiting on God. What changed their minds?

Abraham was about eighty-five. He had been in Canaan ten years. Sarah was ten years younger. Since she lived to be 127, she was a little past middle age according to her lifespan. Most likely past menopause. Physically having children was no longer an option for her. Genesis 16:1 reads like an accusation. "Now Sarai Abram's wife bare him no children."

Surely Abraham had told her of God's promise that a child would be born to him, that Eliezer was not to be considered as an heir. He must have told her about the stars. Sarah must have wondered at his words. She may have noticed the word uterus. God said a son would be born to Abraham. Doubts and questions must have plagued her mind as this time of her life overtook her. She must have felt hollow when she realized her hopes of giving birth were over.

We read her story and know she was relying on her body not God when she thought this; that she was elevating her circumstances over God's words to Abraham. All she knew was her circumstances said her body was passed childbearing.

But then there was Hagar. She was Sarah's Egyptian servant, perhaps included in the slaves given to them when Sarah was kidnapped. Clearly

---

[7] John Bright, *A History of Israel* (Westminster:John Knox Press 2000) pg 79.

God was pointing to another woman to provide an heir for Abraham. Sarah decided to share her position as Abraham's wife, to humble herself and provide for her husband. "And Sarai said unto Abram, Behold now, the LORD hath restrained me from bearing: I pray thee, go in unto my maid; it may be that I may obtain children by her."

Abraham agreed. It seems he took Sarah's offer as God's promised provision. The ease of it looked good to him. It was legal, respectable. Surely this was God. But he too was allowing circumstances to lead them instead of remaining in a place of depending on God's word, bowel and uterus. They both took the bait the culture of the day offered them. It was a subtle misstep with big consequences. This would have been a good time for Abraham to ask God questions and not rush, but desire outweighed caution.

In 2017 *The Times of Israel* ran a story on the discovery of an Assyrian cuneiform tablet of a marriage contract. The contract was similar to the arrangement Sarah made with Hagar. Sarah had said maybe God was going to give her children through Hagar. Either she wasn't convinced this was going to work out or she wondered if it were Abraham who couldn't have children. The answer came quickly. Hagar was pregnant. But she wasn't wise.

Hagar failed to see her position. She had been elevated by her boss, a privilege for sure, but one given to her. She became overly secure as the mother of Abraham's child, forgetting she was the secondary wife. Her son would be given to Sarah to raise, to adopt and become an heir to one of the richest men in Canaan. This was the process of legitimizing the child of a slave in the Ancient Near East. Otherwise, the child was not an heir.[8] Sarah had already considered making this child a legitimate heir. Instead of being grateful, Hagar became arrogant.

---
[8] Paulissian, Adoption.

There was a clause included in laws concerning slave concubines. If a slave given to a man as a concubine became pregnant, that slave could not mock the legal wife. If she did, the primary wife could strip her of her status as secondary wife and make her a slave again.[9] Hagar must have figured Sarah would do nothing to defend herself. She must have known Abraham wouldn't defend Sarah either.

So Hagar mocked. "And he went in unto Hagar, and she conceived: and when she saw that she had conceived, her mistress was despised in her eyes." (Genesis 16:4)

But Sarah did protest. For the first time we see her laying the blame for her unjust treatment at the feet of Abraham. She appealed to God for vindication. "And Sarai said unto Abram, My wrong be upon thee: I have given my maid into thy bosom; and when she saw that she had conceived, I was despised in her eyes: the LORD judge between me and thee."

Wrong is *châmâs* (huhMAS), a cruel, unrighteous, violence, injustice or damage. It is the same word used in Genesis 6:11 to describe the violence before the flood. We spell it *hamas* and see the word used for the Harakat al-Muqawama al-Islamiya, the Islamic Resistance Movement or Hamas. According to etymologist Ernest Klein the word has links to *hamasu* the Akkadian word for oppression.[10] It also has word and meaning associations in Aramaic and Arabic. None of the meanings mean something else other than evildoing or robbery as its meanings in Hebrew describe it.

Despised is *qâlal* (kuLAL), to make small, trifling or light. Hagar was not only mocking in the English sense, she seems to have been attacking Sarah's position violently in an oppressive way. Judge is *shâphat*

---

[9] John Van Seters, "The Problem of Childlessness in near Eastern Law and the Patriarchs of Israel," *Journal of Biblical Literature* 87, no. 4 (1968) pg 403.

[10] Shoshana Kordova, "Word of the Day / Hamas: The Terror Movement That Didn't Do Its Hebrew Homework," *Haaretz*, August 4, 2014.

(shuFAT), to condemn, vindicate, punish or pronounce sentence upon.

But Hagar was right. Abraham said nothing to her. Instead he said the obvious: Hagar was Sarah's maid; Sarah had the right to do whatever she wanted.

To understand Sarah's reaction, let's consider what she may have been feeling. Sarah wanted support, but she didn't get it in the way she had hoped. She wanted protection, but the only person she could rely on was God. She wanted justice for years of shame and humiliation. Years of knowing how Abraham needed an heir. Now God was giving him one... by an insolent slave from Egypt, a place she remembered in her nightmares. She had humbled herself, and offered her husband her slave.

At least she may have thought she humbled herself. She didn't know it yet, but real humility was depending on God's promise. It wasn't providing by her own hand through the world's way of doing things.

Sarah had every right to demote Hagar back to a slave. She even had legal room to see that she was punished. But Sarah's frustration boiled over, and through her own rebellious stupidity, Hagar bore the brunt of it. "And when Sarai dealt hardly with her, she fled from her face." (Genesis 16:6)

The word *'ânâh* is translated dealt hardly. It is the equivalent of brow beat (speak harshly), depress, afflict, humble, chasten or submit. Hagar must have never been treated like this before. She was definitely debased and humiliated, the very treatment she had offered Sarah. She was restored to the position of a slave. And, she realized Abraham wasn't going to bail her out. So Hagar ran away.

Another fact of ancient Babylonian and Nuzi laws dealing with slaves was that runaways could be killed. Anyone who helped her could also be punished. One punishment for runaway slaves was to blind them, reducing them to the lowest level of slavery, that of chattel. Hagar had run away with the future heir inside her. What was the punishment for that?

Notice God calls Hagar Sarah's slave. "And the angel of the LORD found her by a fountain of water in the wilderness, by the fountain in the way to Shur. And he said, Hagar, Sarai's maid, whence camest thou? and whither wilt thou go?" (Genesis 16:7-8)

Hagar might have decided not to be a slave anymore by leaving Sarah, but a slave was what she had made of herself by her behavior. It was her place; she had no reason for pride. It is interesting God does not criticize Sarah's treatment of her. He tells Hagar to return and submit to her mistreatment.

This may seem odd to us. But when God made His promise to Abraham, He told him those who blessed him He [God] would bless and those who cursed him He [God] would curse. Abraham and Sarah were one in God's eyes, something they had forgotten when it came to God's promise about an heir. God had not forgotten. Truly, Hagar made the wrong decision when she decided to mess with Sarah.

But God was not without mercy, even concerning a young woman without much sense. When God told her how He would bless her, He described a son a lot like his mother. "And he will be a wild man; his hand will be against every man, and every man's hand against him; and he shall dwell in the presence of all his brethren." (Genesis 16:12)

Abraham was eighty-six when Ishmael was born. Thirteen years passed with no word from God. Abiding by the current custom may have seemed like a good idea. But Hagar was not God's idea. Strife and division had come upon Abraham's household. The Bible tells us where there is strife there is confusion and evil work. (James 1:3)

But Abraham was satisfied. He had a son. He may have wondered at God's silence as he enjoyed fatherhood and praised God. Sarah may have cared for the baby. But there was always Hagar nearby. Sarah's life was nothing as she had imagined it would be.

Finally God appeared to Abraham. His first words were not the friendly greetings of before. God had never intervened to stop Abraham from taking Hagar as a concubine. He respected his free will to make decisions. That is why it is so critical for us to walk closely with God.

Abraham had one desire at this stage of his life: he wanted an heir. He jumped at what he thought was God providing for him without bothering to ask if Hagar was the plan. He was desperate and it looked like his answer.

By the way, when scholars talk about the possibility of Abraham adopting Sarah in a wife-sister adoption, they are referring to loop holes used to get around ancient laws about inheritance. A person could adopt someone so they could inherit property when otherwise it was illegal or the property was in jeopardy. In his desire for a son and mention of Eliezer, it is not likely that Abraham adopted Sarah.

Abraham had made a big mistake in listening to Sarah and not God. We only assume Sarah knew about Abraham's last conversation with God about having a child. But if she knew God meant her body was the one giving birth to the heir, she gave up on those words. She honored her circumstances more and gave them more weight than the word spoken to Abraham.

The stern greeting is addressed to Abraham, however. "And when Abram was ninety years old and nine, the LORD appeared to Abram, and said unto him, I am the Almighty God; walk before me, and be thou perfect." (Genesis 17:1)

Perfect is *tâmîym* (tahMEEM), whole, without blemish, undefiled. Noah had been called perfect in his generation. God picked Noah because he walked with Him. Abraham had to learn how to walk. When God appeared to him at ninety-nine, He was emphatic Abraham get it right, wholehearted and blameless the *Amplified Bible* says.

Abraham had to choose the authority speaking into his life. Was it going to be the traditions of the world, its laws and customs, or God's word? So far in Abraham's life it had been a mixed bag. This was a warning encouragement. Yes, you read that right. Warning encouragement. Kind of like a firm reminder. God was telling Abraham he had strayed, and God was expecting it wouldn't happen again. This was a critical point in Abram's life. There was a covenant between him and God.

God repeated His promise of multiplying Abraham into a great nation, but this time Abraham was overcome by the presence of God and collapsed. The word used is *nâphal* (naFAL) the same word used as slay, die overwhelm, lie prostrate. It seems God wasn't fooling around, and Abraham experienced God's powerful Spirit.

Then God changed Abraham's identity. We have called him Abraham since we began our study of his life. But if you noticed, the verses from Genesis up to now have all called him Abram, the name Terah gave him. He had been exalted father. The name of Abraham meant the same thing, but by adding the letter corresponding to h, God was extending the decree to include a multitude.

Also, the name change meant an official change of authority over Abraham. Parents name children. Terah, acting as the authority and father figure in Abraham's life had given him the name Abram. But God, now his authority and Father, gave him the purpose for his name. Abraham was to become the father of a multitude and the father of nations. These were two different distinctions, one seen in the Old Testament, one in the New.

It is significant that God said He had made Abraham the father of nations, past tense. It was already done in God's eyes. As God thought so shall it be declares Isaiah 14:24. The word translated made is *nâthan*, which is a primitive root meaning give or ascribe. In other words, God was bearing the burden of multiplying one son into a multitude then a nation. He had *given* this to Abraham. It was crucial for Abram to understand this in his heart so he could be Abraham in the land of Canaan, not just in the mind of God.

Sarah also underwent a name change. Sarai meant "my princess" as she was named by whoever gave her a name, Terah, Haran or someone else. Whoever they were, she was no longer their princess. She was "princess" as an absolute identity in God. She was appointed to be the mother of kings. Thus, God, her authority, gave purpose to her name.

In this encounter God reestablished the promise of Canaan to Abraham, adding that it was to be Abraham's possession forever exactly like the agreement between them. God also presented something new: He wanted Abraham to circumcise himself and every male born or bought in his household. This was to be God's covenant with Abraham and his offspring. His children would carry a mark on their body as a sign of their continuing covenant with God. Circumcision is the removal of a male's foreskin.

"And I will establish my covenant between me and thee and thy seed after thee in their generations for an everlasting covenant, to be a God unto thee, and to thy seed after thee... This is my covenant, which ye shall keep, between me and you and thy seed after thee; Every man child among you shall be circumcised." (Genesis 17:7,10)

Circumcision was not new in the Ancient Near East. Egyptians practiced partial male circumcision, a removal of part of the skin. Images depicting circumcision were discovered on walls in Egypt dating to Djedkare of the Fifth Dynasty. These images prompt scholars to say the Hebrews copied the Egyptians.

But the first evidence of the complete removal of the foreskin was thought to be a scene on an Egyptian palette of naked Semitic captives, bearded men, being attacked by a lion and eaten by vultures.[11] It is an odd scene for a surface used to mix cosmetics, but this particular palette may have been ceremonial and not for everyday use. The Semitic captives were circumcised. It dates to the Gerzeh Period, the era just before the First Dynasties in Egypt, traditionally 3500-3200 BC. All these time periods are in the frame various scholars set Abraham and his family.

Professor Jack Sasson referred to another archaeological find in Syria that suggested circumcision did not originate in Egypt but the Amuq valley.[12] The Amuq valley stretches from the Tigris and Euphrates River basins to the Mediterranean Sea near the Syria Turkey border and near the other ancient cities we've talked about. It is a flat plain with uncommonly large settlements dating back 6,000 years or at least to the earliest of Noah's relatives. The ancient metal industry was big business in this area. Bronze statues dating to 3200 BC were discovered showing circumcised men with beards. Their circumcisions were not partial. They were complete.

During the Pre-dynasty era, the Egyptians were battling foreigners, obviously Semites from the north if the lion and the vultures mean anything, to establish their empire and the god Horus as supreme. Dr. Sasson thinks these northern foreigners influenced Egyptians to practice a type of circumcision. But the real proof is in the language. The word for circumcision in Egyptian mimics the sound of the Hebrew word. It might be evidence of who is copying whom.

But why would God use circumcision to mark another covenant with Abraham?

---

[11] Jean Capart, *Primitive Art in Egypt* (London:H. Grevel & Co. 1905) Fig 179, pg 240, NYU Digital Library.

[12] Jack M. Sasson, "Circumcision In The Ancient Near East," *Journal of Biblical Literature*, 85.4, 1966, 473-476.

The key may be in God's first words to Abraham and His silence for the previous thirteen years. Perfect also means undefiled. Abraham had defiled God's plan by making his own. Having relations with Hagar was a legitimate way of having children according to societal laws and customs, but God deals inside a different kingdom. Hagar as an Egyptian was not part of God's plan for Abraham's offspring. Like the Egyptians adapted circumcision, making it partial instead of complete, Abraham had adapted God's plan to fit his own.

For Abraham it needed to be complete. Romans 12:1 begs us to offer our bodies as a living sacrifice, holy and acceptable to God. Perhaps Abraham's circumcision was a reminder that complete obedience was obedience and included every part of the body. Every Israelite male would have the sign on their body as a reminder of whose they were and where they came from. This covenant, God said, would be in their flesh as an everlasting covenant. Every slave born or bought would know for whom they had been set apart, a possession of Yahweh, the God of Abraham. This covenant would mark the nation of Israel.

Let's interrupt the flow of the story for a moment to analyze an example of a scholar misinterpreting the Bible. Gerald A. Larue was a minister who became an atheist focused on discrediting the Bible. He was involved in a hoax concerning Noah's ark in which he set out to prove the [supposed] absurd willingness of many in the Christian community to believe anything. Unfortunately he ignored the plethora of real science concerning Noah. And, he ignored real history when it came to the rest of the Old Testament.

For instance, he wrote, "The earliest reference to circumcision in the Bible is in a folk-tale (written prior to Genesis 17) associated with Moses."[13] In this statement Larue claims Genesis was written after the

---

[13] Gerald A. Larue, "Religious Traditions and Circumcision," The Second International

Exodus which it was by Moses. Moses told us that. No surprises there. But the written histories of Genesis were recorded in the *towlĕdahs*, stating "this is the history of." These records were written and kept carefully as archaeology has proven through the Nuzi Tablets.[14] The fact that Moses used records was stated in the Bible and is supported by evidence dating to the same time.

Larue was also telling us he believed the story wasn't true. After quoting the verses in the Bible where Zipporah circumcised her son, he writes, "This strange insertion into the tenth century B.C.E. temple fiction about Moses suggests that circumcision became Hebrew custom through contact with the Midianites... A still later tradition (post-sixth century B.C.E.) traced Hebrew circumcision back to Abraham..."[15]

Larue mistakenly said the first reference to Hebrew circumcision was about Moses whom he considered a myth. Notice the years he used, 900-400 BC. He believes the Old Testament was written while the Jews were in Babylon. Since he refused to recognize that the *towlĕdahs* in Genesis were ancient histories Moses collected and preserved, Larue missed the authentic first mention of Hebrew circumcision, Abraham's, and therefore missed its meaning. When the Bible is isolated from its original, authentic history, it looses meaning.

The point is Larue made a decision to ignore any possibility of biblical authenticity and wrote his own history based on the belief that the Bible is fiction. This is an example of opinions following an assumption. But when Larue based his assumptions on a false foundation, he had to ignore a lot of truth to continue in that path. And he did, as he continued to write against later archaeological finds.

Abraham's covenant of circumcision has no meaning outside of
Symposium on Circumcision, San Francisco, California, April 30-May 3, 1991.

[14] "What Noah Knew," *NOAH*, Flying Eagle Publications, pg 6.
[15] Larue, Religious Traditions

its historical place and separated from historical people. Like Larue, there are many who are puzzled by its purpose. They only give a medical reason or list possible health benefits of circumcision. Some think Abraham had to be circumcised so Sarah could become pregnant. As if that matters to a woman who has experienced menopause.

Sarah was still God's chosen mother of the nation He desired. But Sarah's and Abraham's complete obedience was required. God gave her a new name to help strengthen her trust. This time God made it plain to Abraham Sarah was to be the mother of the child, so plain he laughed.

She had never had children. And he was almost a hundred years old. This was impossible. But God's promise was clear and firmly repeated. "And God said unto Abraham, As for Sarai thy wife, thou shalt not call her name Sarai, but Sarah shall her name be. And I will bless her, and give thee a son also of her: yea, I will bless her, and she shall be a mother of nations; kings of people shall be of her." (Genesis 17:15-16)

God declared He was going to bless Sarah. He was going to do the work of opening her womb to give her a child. It wouldn't be Abraham's effort or ability or Sarah's. It was totally through the grace of God.

But Abraham didn't really get it. He didn't understand that his promise wasn't coming through Egypt by way of Ishmael. He asked God to bless Ishmael, apparently instead of the crazy idea of he and Sarah having a baby.

Abraham had raised Ishmael for the last thirteen years as the heir and beginning of a nation. Abraham thought he was the promised son. It must have been a shock to find out he wasn't. This son he loved, to whom he had poured out his heart and knowledge with high hopes, was not God's chosen? Abraham was not fond of God's plan. It seemed too hard. Besides, he already had a son.

But God said, "Sarah thy wife shall bear thee a son indeed; and thou shalt call his name Isaac: and I will establish my covenant with him for an everlasting covenant, and with his seed after him." (Genesis 17:19)

God wasn't punishing Ishmael. He would be blessed. The child God called Isaac, however, was the one with whom God wanted to confirm the covenant because his mother would be Sarah. It wasn't God's fault Abraham and Sarah took the burden to provide for them and went outside God's plan to do so.

There are those who see joy not unbelief in Abraham's laugh. It may be interpreted either way and still make sense. But if it were joy, there may not have been the need for another conversation in Genesis 18.

Abraham immediately circumcised himself and the men of his house. Somehow the practice even got over to Lot, because his descendants circumcised their males. We do not know why.

But Abraham must have never told Sarah that God said she was going to have a baby. In Genesis 18 three visitors came to stand near Abraham's tent under the oaks of Mamre. One of the visitors was the Lord Jesus. "And the LORD appeared unto him in the plains of Mamre." (Genesis 18:1) Sarah was inside, but it was hot, and Abraham sat in the doorway. When he saw the visitors, he greeted them and arranged for a meal to be prepared.

It was while the men were eating under the trees that the Lord asked about Sarah using her new name. "And they said unto him, Where is Sarah thy wife?" (Genesis 18:9) Of course God already knew even though the tent was behind him. She was inside the family home. The old Hebrew pictograph for the letter *beyt* looks like this ⌂ , and is a representation of the interior of the tent home. *Beyt* is also a Hebrew word meaning home.[16]

---

[16] Jeff A. Benner, "The Goat Hair Tent of the Hebrew Nomads" *Ancient Hebrew Research Center.*

The women's section was on the right. Sometimes there was a third section for servants. Women could also have their own tent like Rachel and Leah. But Sarah was standing in the doorway, either between her section and Abraham's or the front entrance.

It was the first time God singled her out, and it was significant. If Abraham hadn't told her about her name change and having a baby, God was telling her Himself. If Abraham had told her and she didn't believe it, God was letting her hear it firsthand.

Her head must have jerked up when the Lord called her by her new name. What man would do such a thing? He also gave her more encouragement. He told her when she could expect her son to be born. "And he said, I will certainly return unto thee according to the time of life; and, lo, Sarah thy wife shall have a son." (Genesis 18:10)

But Sarah couldn't imagine such a thing. It was ridiculous! Wasn't it? She laughed. Was it a bitter laugh? Probably.

"And the LORD said unto Abraham, Wherefore did Sarah laugh, saying, Shall I of a surety bear a child, which am old?"

Why did God comment about her laughing? He didn't say anything to Abraham when he laughed in Genesis 17:17. For Abraham, it may have been a reprimand. Why doesn't she believe, Abraham? Perhaps God had to change what Abraham thought about Sarah as much as He had to change what Sarah thought about herself. Or, God was prodding Abraham to work at building Sarah's faith.

Either way, Abraham had to rid himself of the settled attitude of his affairs. He had to reconsider what he did not think was valuable: his wife and his own body. He had to let go of the dreams he held for Ishmael.

Some wonder why Abraham was so concerned about fathering a child at a hundred when his own father had a son (Abraham) at 130.

But something was happening to people in Abraham's day. They were dying younger and probably aging faster than previous generations.

God corrected Sarah's thoughts because He knew her heart. She hadn't had the easiest life. She had a long time for discouragement to set in. She had watched while others gained because of her sacrifices. Her arms ached for her own child as much as Abraham's had. But she was empty. Or so she thought.

God had known her name. He had never given up desiring her to be His chosen vessel for a chosen nation. She had purpose. Even when her time of promise had passed. He knew her inmost thoughts. He had repeated the doubts running through her mind. Why laugh, He asked her. So He gave her something else to replace her doubt: "Is any thing too hard for the LORD? At the time appointed I will return unto thee, according to the time of life, and Sarah shall have a son." (Genesis 18:14)

According to the time of life means the season. Sarah had a lot to feed her confident expectation and imagination. By the same time the following year, she would be having her son.

Sarai poured water over her hands and wiped them on her dress. "Ishmael!" she called, motioning for him to join her. "Here." She pressed a wooden ladle of water into his hands.

The lad gulped the water. "Wa-na and I are practicing with our bows."

Sarai nodded. "I see that. But it is time to rest. Tell your stories in the shade among the goats."

"Mother Hagar says I do not have to rest. I am strong for the desert."

"We are not living in a desert. And she does not have to move sheep with your father this evening does she? I am her mother too, and you must listen to me, Ishmael. You do not honor yourself with such talk."

The boy frowned but took another drink as Sarai offered it. She watched him trot off towards Wa-na or Yonah as she called him. The boys would sit in the shade for awhile before Ishmael would disregard her instructions, she thought.

Sarai entered the cool tent and sat at her weaving. She heard Abraham come to sit at his place in the doorway. They didn't talk much together. Not like the early days. So much promise then. Promise. Her stomach lurched at the word. It was all about Ishmael now. She was an outsider.

She tore the strands apart and started again. She wasn't angry anymore. Just...Just done, she decided. With everything.

Abraham rose suddenly and hurried away. She stood and peered outside the tent. Visitors.

"Quickly," Abram told her as he returned. "Make bread. I will go have Mika-el prepare a calf."

"Curds. Bring curds," she answered as he left. She glanced at the visitors and began to gather the flour.

Later as the men ate their meal under the trees, she sat again at her *weaving stool. Ishmael had not come back with Abram. Which meant, she told herself, he was no where near the trees of Mamre. She made a face.*

"*Where is your wife, Sarah?*"

She tip toed to the doorway as Abram replied. The man sat with his back to her. Why didn't Abram correct this man's error? Her name wasn't Sarah. She stared at the rug on the floor as the visitor spoke again. His words... His words sounded so authoritative. But insensible. Hadn't this prophet seen her? She was too old to have a baby. And Abram. There he was right in front of the man! He was even older. Some prophet.

She laughed into her cupped hands. A child? Me?

"*Why did Sarah laugh and say 'Can I have a child when I am old?' Is anything too hard for the Lord?*"

Sarai dropped to her knees as the words hit her. Instantly visions of Pharaoh loomed in her mind. The hopelessness of Egypt, but God had heard her. He had seen and delivered her when she had no one else. Hagar's insults burned again in her ears. But God had protected her position. She had not been cast down or divorced as useless. God had seen her now and knew her thoughts.

"*I will return and Sarah will have a son.*"

The words entered her ears and brought life with them, carrying deep into her heart. Sarah shall have a son.

She swallowed but her throat had gone dry. "*My Lord, I did not laugh,*" *she said gripping her skirt.*

"*Yes. You did.*"

Sarai closed her eyes as tears ran down her face. All the bitterness left as she heaved silent sobs. She thought of the years Abram had looked upon her with sadness. Every month passing without hope. Until he no longer looked. He no longer expected. And finally it was over.

But this man's words. His words came from the heart of God.

"Forgive me, God," she breathed.

No longer would she be a reproach. She would have no more shame. Is anything too hard for the Lord?

"No, Lord," she whispered. *"With You nothing is impossible. I believe. I am Sarah. Your princess and noble woman, and I receive Your power to have a child."*

❖ ❖ ❖

The Lord's eyes bore into Abraham as he spoke Sarai's name. He had called her Sarah. He had also called her his wife. It felt like a reminder. Was it a rebuke? He had stopped thinking about her that way. Why would the Lord ask about her?

"Why did Sarah laugh?"

Abraham could make no reply. He had cast the words concerning Sarai having a child aside. She wasn't able, he had thought. He knew it now and so did everyone else. But his spirit quickened at the word laugh. Isaac. It was to be the boy's name. The Lord had told him before and here was the word again. He and Sarai had both laughed… The Lord was watching him.

"Is there anything too hard for the Lord?"

The words sank into his chest. Could he really have another son? With Sarai?

Something stirred in the depths of his belly. Hope. He stared into the Lord's eyes. Sarah shall have a son. The thought grew stronger. Relief settled onto his shoulders and a smile crept across his lips. It was done. They had a son.

The Lord smiled back.

Chapter 7
Sodom and Ishmael: Paying the Piper

The biblical account of Sodom and Gomorrah is discredited by many modern scholars. Its visitation by angels and destruction by God is too big a supernatural pill to swallow. Lot's story is shelved with Greek myths like *Baucis and Philemon* written by Ovid in Book VIII Fable VI in *Metamorphosis*. It is assumed and decided the Bible copied this type of myth.

But Ovid, Publius Ovidius Naso as he was named, was born about 43 BC. Lot's story was written much earlier as the Dead Sea Scrolls prove. Skeptics date the Old Testament to around 600 BC. So, by their own dating methods, who copied whom? It cannot be stated logically that Lot is inspired by Ovid's poem.

It may be argued that the story of a god visiting his creation and deciding to destroy it circulated through all ancient cultures, and a Christian would not disagree. But they know the I AM God of the Bible was the god. In fact in Ovid's story, Zeus and Hermes destroy the village with a flood, not fire. Ovid's story is a mixture of Noah and Lot whose accounts predate Ovid's. It is truly a metamorphosis, a change from one thing into a completely different thing: from truth to a lie.

When the three visitors arrived at Abraham's camp, they weren't on a sight-seeing trip. The Lord never does anything without a purpose and He never wastes words.

On His way out of the Oaks of Mamre, the Lord turned toward Sodom and asked a question. "Shall I hide from Abraham that thing which I do..." (Genesis 18:17) The phrasing sounds funny as it translates into modern English. But whom did He ask? Certainly not the two angels with Him. In the New Testament, Jesus said He only spoke what the Father told Him to speak. (John 12:49) Scholars believe He was consulting the Heavenly Father.

The Lord also continued to speak encouragement to Abraham about having more children. It is a great lesson on decreeing a thing like in Job 22:28, or speaking the end from the beginning like in Isaiah 46:9-10. In Abraham's presence, this is what the Lord spoke:

> Shall I hide from Abraham that thing which I do seeing that Abraham shall surely become a great and mighty nation, and all the nations of the earth shall be blessed in him? For I know him, that he will command his children and his household after him, and they shall keep the way of the LORD, to do justice and judgment; that the LORD may bring upon Abraham that which he hath spoken of him. (Genesis 18:17-19)

Then the Lord announced He was on His way to Sodom. He had heard some bad reports and was going to check it out. If it was as bad as the angels had reported when they came before Him, He was going to have it destroyed. Of course God already knew it was, the same way He knew about what was happening at the Tower of Babel. But God is personal, and here he made a personal visit with two witnesses.

Critics of the Bible think the story of Sodom and Gomorrah is proof God is unfair. Actually, Satan may not have liked that God would destroy his hotbeds of perversion from time to time, like at the flood. But to address the critics, the few times God stepped in to assert His authority was to stop sin.

And Sodom was famous for its sin. Most think of Sodom and think homosexuality, and while that is true, the Bible lists a progression of sins in which the last, called abominations, were fed and produced by pride, abundance and lack of compassion towards the poor.

> Behold, this was the iniquity of thy sister Sodom, pride, fulness of bread, and abundance of idleness was in her and in her daughters, neither did she strengthen the hand of the poor and needy. And they were haughty, and committed abomination before me: therefore I took them away as I saw good. (Ezekiel 16:49-50)

It is important to note the word translated idleness is *shâqat* (shuh-CAT). This is an idleness that appeases, is not disturbed and remains quiet. In essence, no one was bothered by the goings on in Sodom.

Abraham couldn't believe God would destroy righteous people, of whom he was probably thinking of Lot, so he bargained God down to ten people. This is the trait in Abraham scholars insist makes him a traveling salesman. The truth is, God couldn't even find ten people, but He saved Lot and his family anyway. That is good news for anyone praying for family members.

It is boring to repeat, but this is their story and they are sticking to it: many scholars believe Sodom and Gomorrah is merely a literary tale like Aesop's Fables to teach a lesson. And, this really is tiresome, the stories may have been inserted later because we all know Abraham is dated to the Middle Bronze Age and there was no one living in Sodom and Gomorrah then. In fact, the towns probably never existed.

You know what comes next...

There are three theories— besides the one that they don't exist. The first theory is the cities are under the Dead Sea. The second is they are west of the Dead Sea. The third is they are somewhere east of the Dead Sea. Most important, what does the Bible say about the cities?

Genesis 10:19 lists towns forming Canaan's border. Five of these towns are east of the Dead Sea: Sodom, Gomorrah, Admah, Zeboiim and Lasha (*lesha'* boiling spring).[1] Lasha was later called Callirhoe, according to the ancient historian Jerome, and was famous for its hot springs. Another ancient historian, Eusebius put it near Sodom.

Zoar or Bela is missing from the list in Genesis 10, but it was a new city in Abraham's time. You may recognize four of the names from our study of Genesis 14 when Abraham helped the five cities of the plain.

Excavations at Tall el-Hammam by Dr. Steven Collins have convinced him that he has found the site of ancient Sodom. He says the site, northeast of Jerusalem, has twenty-five "geographic indicators" that match the biblical location.[2] He dates the site to 1700 BC, a time he says fits perfectly with the dating of Abraham to the Middle Bronze Age. He wrote a best-selling book highlighting his research and discovery.

Another recent article concerning Tall el-Hammam seems to support Dr. Collins' theory. *Newsweek* and other news outlets published a story about an asteroid being responsible for destroying Sodom and its neighboring cities.[3]

---

[1] Mt. Nebo is on the eastern border where Moses had to stop because he could not enter the Promised Land.

[2] Brian Nixon, "More Evidence Confirms Tall el-Hammam as Sodom," *Assist News Service*. August 21, 2018.

[3] Katherine Highnett, "Biblical City Of Sodom Was Blasted To Smithereens By A Massive Asteroid Explosion," *Newsweek*, November 22, 2018.

But this northern location for Sodom is debated for many reasons. One, it is north of the location for Sodom listed in other verses of the Bible such as Genesis 14 and Abraham's battle in the Valley of Siddim (Salt Sea). Ezekiel 16:46 puts Sodom south of Jerusalem, not northeast. Two, the supposed discoveries are in the wrong time period. Abraham dates to the Early Bronze Age not the Middle. Three, the geography is not as compelling as Dr. Collins proposes. In fact it directly contradicts historical and archaeological references to the cities. His work is still important. It just doesn't fit Sodom, however.

The traditional site for Sodom and Gomorrah is east of the Jordan River and the Dead Sea. The city of Zoar, where Lot fled to escape the destruction, was inhabited until the Middle Ages. There are numerous extra-biblical sources mentioning Zoar and its location south of the Dead Sea and east of the Jordan. Josephus, an ancient Jewish historian, described a lake he called Asphaltitis which is the Dead Sea and said it stretched as far as Zoar in Arabia. He said Sodom was in the area but had been destroyed.

Zoar was located in the Roman province of *Palaestina Salutaris* in an area covering south of the Dead Sea, the Negev and Petra. Eusebius, who was born around 260 AD and died around 340 AD, wrote a dictionary of ancient place names called *Onomasticon*. He translated the Hebrew *Tsô'ar* (Zoar) into Greek as Zogera, Zogora, Segor and Sigor and said it was one of the five cities of the plain, referring to Genesis 14. He also put it south of the Dead Sea.

Around four decades after Eusebuius' death, a wealthy woman named Egeria traveled throughout the Holy Land. She wrote to her girlfriends about the bishop of Zoara. And so it goes all the way to the time of the Crusades when Zoar was called Palmer and recognized for its delicious dates by famous archbishops like William of Tyre and Arabic mapmakers.

Speaking of maps, the oldest map of the Holy Land is made out of tiles and laid out on the floor of St. George's church in Madaba, Jordan.[4] The mosaic was created between 542-570 AD and has been proven by archaeology to be a reliable source of information.

Less than a hundred years after it was created, the area was conquered by Muslims and part of the map was defaced. In later years, an earthquake, water damage and other hazards took their toll. When it was rediscovered in the late 1800s, a church was built over it.

What is interesting about the map is Madaba is the city of Medeba first mentioned in Numbers 21. Medeba is a Moabite town. Moab was the son of Lot, so we do not find it surprising to see Zoar on the mosaic map in the region where Lot's family settled after Sodom was destroyed.

Zoar is shown on the east side of the Dead Sea near modern day Safi, Jordan, a little below Wadi Hesa. The Sanctuary of St. Lot is nearby, built around the mouth of a cave. Genesis 19:30 says, "And Lot went up out of Zoar, and dwelt in the mountain, and his two daughters with him; for he feared to dwell in Zoar: and he dwelt in a cave, he and his two daughters." If you are adventurous, you can visit the cave today near Safi.

Even non-biblical scholars may confidently place Zoar south of the Dead Sea. It is also important to realize Zoar is about sixty miles south of Dr. Collins' northern location for Sodom. Lot had complained he couldn't run to the mountains because they were too far. Collins' theory places Zoar farther from Sodom than the mountains.

>And Lot said to them, Oh no, Lord, please now,
>Your servant has found grace in Your sight, and You

---

[4] The church was named St. George after an elite soldier in the Roman Praetorian Guard. The soldier was killed for being a Christian. There is an interesting legend about him called Saint George and the Dragon.

have magnified Your mercy, which You have shown to me in saving my life. And I cannot escape to the mountain, lest some evil take me and I die. Behold now, this city is near to flee to, and it is a little one. Oh let me escape there (is it not a little one?) and my soul shall live. Genesis 19:18-20

To sum up, the Bible and other sources indicate Sodom was nearer to Zoar than Dr. Collins' proposed location northeast of Jerusalem.

Isaiah 15:5 says Moab's fugitives would run to Zoar. Jeremiah said calamity in Moab would even reach Zoar, eliminating any refuge. So why was everyone fleeing to Zoar? Were they just copying Lot?

Zoar and its other name Bela means little in Hebrew. At the time of Lot it was the smaller city. But it became a larger town after the others were destroyed. It was thought to be one of the trade cities connecting Arabia to the north and became important and well supplied.

Archaeologists have found the largest ancient cemetery north of Zoar at Khirbet Qazone. Over 5,000 ancient Jewish burials have been discovered. The earliest burials date to the Early Bronze Age, which you know by now was the time of Lot and Abraham. Today modern homes built over the site prevent further excavations.

According to history, this area east of the Dead Sea is where the other original cities of the plain were located. Among the Ebla Tablets is a tablet listing trade cities and routes. It describes one route south through the central hill country of modern day Israel, along the west shore of the Dead Sea and then circling its southern edge to travel north along the eastern shore. Two cities are named on the eastern side: Admah and Sodom.[5]

---

[5] Bryant G. Wood, "Discovery of the Sin Cities of Sodom and Gomorrah." Associates for Biblical Research. April 16, 2008.

Ancient historians like Tacitus, Philo and Strabo write of the existence of cities near Sodom that were destroyed by an earthquake. Beginning in 1965, excavations in this area of modern day Jordan revealed Early Bronze Age cities.

Walter E. Rast and Thomas Schaub, both professors and archaeologists, excavated the sites of Bâb edh-Dhrâ' and Numeira and co-authored a book about their discoveries. They agreed with earlier research that Bâb edh-Dhrâ' and Numeira dated to the Early Bronze Age, the same time as Zoar. They found Bâb edh-Dhrâ' and Numeira were inhabitated in the Early Bronze Age with Bâb edh-Dhrâ' being the largest site. The city covered almost ten acres.

Rast and Schaub thought these sites may have been cities related to the Genesis 14 account. More excavation work followed and many archaeologists and scholars have concluded Bâb edh-Dhrâ' is ancient Sodom and Numeira is Gomorrah. The Arabic word Numeira even has linguistic ties in its name to Gomorrah. Other sites have been suggested for Admah and Zeboiim, but there is nothing conclusive yet.

Think about the size of Sodom—ten acres— when you read about the threat made to the angels and Lot in Genesis 19:4-5.

> But before they lay down, the men of the city, even the men of Sodom, compassed the house round, both young and old, all the people from every quarter; and they called unto Lot, and said unto him, Where are the men that came in to thee this night? bring them out unto us, that we may know them.

All the men from every part of the city both young and old must have been a good sized mob of men and boys with one thing on their mind. This shows the extent of the violence in Sodom.

The discoveries concerning Sodom and Gomorrah were amazing. There were cities, cultured urban centers, in what seems an odd, out of the way place so early in history. These were not religious sites, but cities with homes and people growing grains, orchards of olives, grapes, peaches and figs. There were signs that some residents were semi-nomadic shepherds. Like Lot. A thick wall surrounded Bâb edh-Dhrâ' and about a thousand people lived there. More lived outside the city.

Today we understand each of the five cities were located by rivers and the well watered land Lot saw was completely irrigated. Lot said it was like the Garden of the Lord, perhaps referring to Eden and the way water came up from the ground to water the plants. Scholars find meaning in the term cities *of* the plain, saying it reveals a bond with the land. *Kikâr* (keeCARH) is translated plain, but it can also mean circle, an image perhaps of the land and its interconnected cites around the shore of the Dead Sea.

The Bible says Lot journeyed east. Sodom was not his immediate destination but he ended up there. What he saw intrigued him, green lush land, an easier life. He moved toward it gradually, leaving behind his uncle's harder life.

In Chapter 5, we learned that the Dead Sea periodically flooded near its southern edge, but in Abraham's lifetime it was dry. Tar pits were scattered in this area and even today signs warn visitors of their presence. Also petroleum and sulfur can be found under the ground nearby. Geologist Frederick Clapp studied this Dead Sea plain in 1929 and 1934. He thought that an earthquake might have destroyed the cities and the volatile chemicals exploded, burning whatever was left.

Modern geologists like Professor Jack Donahue agreed after studying the excavations. Dr. Bryant G. Wood in his article, "The Discovery of the Sin Cities of Sodom and Gomorrah," says Bâb edh-Dhrâ' and

Numeira are sitting on fault lines. By examining the Hebrew language's description of the event, he helps us get a better image of what happened at Sodom.

Our Bibles translate brimstone (sulfur) for the word *gophriyth* (gof REETH). Strong's defines *gophriyth/goprit* as judgment or Jehovah's breath. It also means a resin like substance and sulfur.

Revelation 20:10 says Satan will ultimately be thrown into a lake of this kind of substance that is on fire. The New Testament Greek word for brimstone is *theion* which implies flashing.

According to Wolf Leslau,[6] *goprit* is not a Hebrew word, but he agrees it means sulfur. Jeff Benner from the Ancient Hebrew Research Center translates it as a rock of sulfur that burns. Abraham, the Hebrew eyewitness, seems to be telling us more, however.

Dr. Wood says *goprit* is from the Akkadian *ki/ubritu,* sulfurous oil. This is what exploded from underground and rained on four of the cities. (Zoar was excluded because Lot went there.) Abraham described a thick smoke, like clouds in a thunderstorm *qîytôr (keeTORR)* rising upward like that coming from a kiln, *kibshân* (kivSHON) where smoke is forced out a flue. *Qîytôr* is only used three times in the Bible. It is not the usual word for smoke (*'ashan*).

Obviously Abraham hadn't seen anything like it before. For us it would be similar to the oil fires in Kuwait in 1991. You can watch a video of them on the internet. The landscape was devastated and poisoned at Kuwait. The same happened at Sodom.

The excavations at Bâb edh-Dhrâ' showed walls and towers collapsed violently; fire began on roofs, and as the roofs caved in, fire burned the interior of the buildings. Surprisingly, ash still covers the

---

[6]Wolf Leslau, *Hebrew Cognates In Amharic,* (Wiesbaden:Otto Harrassowitz, 1969), 47.

area. It was in every building uncovered. 2Peter 2:6 tells us Sodom was reduced to ashes, and we have discovered the Bible isn't lying. Respected Bible teacher, Rick Renner points out that the Greek word used for ashes in 2 Peter, *tephroō*, which literally means to incinerate and turn to ashes, was the same word used by Dio Cassius as he described Mt. Vesuvius.[7]

If a person can put any trust in history and archaeology, then they can be confident the Bible has given them an accurate picture of the events at Sodom.

Numeira suffered the same fate as Sodom and at the same time. But some of its residents must have either felt tremors or were in some way warned because there is evidence people packed up food and belongings and left quickly. Dr. Wood described seeing unusually large grape clusters perfectly preserved among the ruins. Perhaps it was a species of grapes like those Moses' spies brought back to the Israelites in Numbers 13.

Dr. Wood points out there was evidence at both sites for a previous destruction. It looked similar to the description of Chedorlaomer's attack about twenty years before. Signs of fire damage on stones and rebuilt walls were found amid the final destruction.

We have learned then that Sodom, Zoar, Admah and Gomorrah were real cities east of the Dead Sea. They are mentioned in several historians' writings and in the trade cities of the Ebla Tablets. Sodom was noted as being destroyed by fire and an earthquake in a cataclysmic event. Sodom and Gomorrah have most likely been located and are Bâb edh-Dhrâ' and Numeira. They both show evidence of two destructions, the last a violent catastrophe.

We have also learned there are some who argue for a northern Sodom and Gomorrah. But this location is in direct opposition to Bible

---

[7] Dio Cassius' description of Mt. Vesuvius' eruption is interesting. His reference to giants may have a layer of truth to it. You can read it online. Look for the link in the Bibliography.

verses. To accept it, means to ignore the Bible and historical references. This theory has recently become popular through news articles about an asteroid and a best selling book. The theory Sodom is under the Sea is not likely if the area was flooded when it was built.

Abraham knew where the cities were. They were part of the land in the Jordan valley God was giving to him. This may have been why God included Abraham in what was happening to the cities and told him why it was happening. No other ancient source besides the Bible gives a spiritual reason for the sudden destruction. But Abraham as well as everyone else in the area probably knew of the cities' reputation.

Which is why we wonder at Lot's settling there. Our reference in 2Peter goes on to say that Lot was righteous but troubled by Sodom's evils. "And He [God] delivered righteous Lot, who had been oppressed by the behavior of the lawless in lustfulness. For that righteous one living among them day after day, in seeing and in hearing, his righteous soul was tormented with their lawless deeds." (2Pe 2: 7-8)

And yet he was sitting at the city gate when the angels walked into Sodom. Sitting at the gate was reserved for the towns' officials. To be a town official meant Lot had to be accommodating of the citizens' values to some degree. His warped sense of right and wrong or his willingness to appease the violent nature of the men of Sodom was obvious when he offered his daughters up for mob torture. The tell-tale sign of his complacency was the angels were forced to grab him and his family and make them leave Sodom.

Where were Lot's sons-in-law? Perhaps with Lot's herds? Or perhaps with the men of the city? Wherever they were, they were left behind.

The angels actually saved Lot's life twice. First from the men of the city who were about to rape and torture him. Genesis 19:9 states, "And they said, Stand back! And they said, This one came in to visit, and must he always judge? Now we will do evil to you rather than to them. And they pressed on the man, upon Lot violently, and drew near to break the door." (LITV) The second time the angels saved Lot was when they took him by the hand and led him out of the city.

But they could do nothing for his character. When Lot chose to journey east, he had no intention of ending up scared, penniless and hiding in a cave near Zoar.

So why does the Bible call Lot righteous? Lot did not commit the sins of Sodom. But he tolerated them enough to live there. Perhaps as one of the town's officials he tried to change Sodom for the better. Instead Sodom affected his reasoning by clouding it. He had lived under the influence of Abraham. He knew what wickedness was, and his conscience bothered him. He did not have peace. Unfortunately, he was too weak to stand against the evil in himself. When he did try to stand, it was a flawed attempt.

When Abraham and Sarah heard about Lot, they may have been saddened. Abraham, however, may have had an inkling of Lot's weaknesses. For whatever reason, he never considered adopting Lot.

Lot's life spiraled downhill after his rescue. Fear seemed to have kept him living in a cave with no future hopes. Fortunately his daughters had been rescued out of Sodom, but the wicked influence of Sodom was not flushed out of them. What the Bible reveals, however, is Lot may have been sorry and asked God's forgiveness later in life. He, like us, was a man of mistakes, big and small, who received God's mercy and was better off because he did.

For Abraham and Sarah life went on. The sulfurous smell of the burning cities may have lingered, but they did not. It was time to move to the Negev. It is said that Abraham lived between Kadesh and Shur. Kadesh is an interesting word. *Qâdêsh* describes a sanctuary for male prostitutes to pagan gods. Ancient historians said it was northeast of Egypt and reached to the territory of the Arabic tribes. Shur means wall and was also northeast of Egypt. How far east either of these was located is debated. As we learned earlier, other scholars admit the possibility of two towns named Kadesh.[8]

After Abraham had lived in the Negev awhile, he moved farther west to Gerar which Genesis 21:32 says is the land of the Philistines. The Philistines were not Canaanites. A recent DNA study of skeletal remains from an ancient Philistine cemetery showed European heritage from across the Mediterranean. Some scientists are skeptical the DNA is pure enough to be trusted. But archaeology has shown a connection to Greek culture and supports the claim.

That is not the whole story, however. Genesis 10:13-14 says the Philistines are related to the Egyptians. Genesis 10:14 states they are descended from Mizraim's son Casluhim. The Masoretic Text says, "... and Casluhim, from whom came the Philistines and Caphtorim." (Genesis 10:14 LITV) Jeremiah 47:4 calls the Philistines remnants of Caphtor.

Josephus says the Caphthorim were overthrown in a war with the Ethiopians, but nothing else is known about their towns. The name of a place called Caphtor is found in tablets at Ugarit, Mari and even Egyptian texts. Amos 9:7 states "... and the Philistines from Caphtor..." .

Some scholars think Caphtor is Crete. But originally scholars saw the Egyptian reference to *Keftiu* and translated it as being a portion of land near the Nile delta. The Akkadians called Caphtor *Kaptara,* and the first instance of the word is in an inscription of Sargon of Akkad. This corresponds to the time of the Old Kingdom in Egypt.

Scholars have many theories, but these cousins of the Egyptians must have mingled with Greeks coming into Canaan. Deuteronomy

---

[8]More discussion on Kadesh can be found in *Moses*, Flying Eagle Publications.

2:23 says the people of Caphtor eventually replaced a people called Avites in Canaan and along the coast from *Hazerim* (villages) down to Gaza *(Azzah)*. Gaza is not far from Gerar where Abraham decided to live for awhile.

Modern scholars state there were no Philistines in Canaan during Abraham's supposed lifetime. But archaeology has uncovered pottery connected to the Egyptian culture in large settlements in the northern Sinai region where the Bible says the Philistines came from. Archaeologists have also noted the same settlements in southern Canaan near the time of the Jemdat Nasr period and First Dynasty of Egypt.[9]

There are extra-biblical sources then putting the Philistines in Canaan, the same place the Bible puts them and at he same time. Historians have learned the Philistines also worshipped Canaanite gods. At the time of Abraham they lived near Gaza and Gerar. Later, at the time of Israel's Judges and early monarchy, they became stronger as Sea Peoples, Greeks, joined them, and they conquered towns from Gaza north to modern day Tel Aviv.

Sometimes people confuse Philistines with Phoenicians. The Phoenicians were Canaanites with a Semitic language. They called themselves *Kenaani*. One of their first cities dating to the early Third Millennium BC was *Gbl*. The Greeks called it Byblos which is in Lebanon. *Gbl* was a city when Abraham entered Canaan. Sidon and Tyre were two other Phoenician cities.

Phoenicians were excellent sailors and traded with many countries, including Egypt, Crete, Cyprus and later Israel. Because they did, their culture reflected Greek influence, and their territory also bordered the Mediterranean coast. They had a lot of things in common with Philistines. Just remember the Phoenicians were Canaanites living in Lebanon and the Philistines were not Canaanites but they moved there.

---

[9] Osgood, "The Times of Abraham."

Abimelech was a Philistine. The term Abi melech is a title that means father king. When Abraham moved to Gerar he met King Abimelech under those awkward circumstances when he told everybody Sarah was his sister. Ancient Gerar is Tel Haror, less than twenty miles from Gaza and northwest of Beersheba.

We have already talked about the incident with Abimelech, but there are a few interesting points we haven't mentioned. To begin with, it was the same ruse they used against Pharaoh, but this time in Gerar Sarah might have been in the early stages of pregnancy. This might explain God's firm warning to Abimelech, "You are a dead man." Also in Gerar, Sarah's beauty may not have been the reason Abimelech took her. Abraham's wealth could have been the reason. Her looks were not mentioned specifically like they were in Egypt.

That idea is only a guess, however. Sarah at ninety could have looked the equivalent of a fifty year old woman in our day since she lived to be 127. Or not. All we know is Sarah was a beautiful woman who just happened to be rich. That was a combination Abimelech couldn't resist.

In God's conversation with Abimelech, he called Abraham a prophet for the first time. The King of Gerar was impressed and fearful. His life and those of his house depended on Abraham's prayer. If Abimelech's motive was gaining Abraham's wealth, it cost him much more to pay for his sin against Abraham and Sarah.

Later, Abimelech would visit Abraham to make a covenant agreement with him. Isaac had been born by the time of Abimelech's covenant which may have prompted the king's words, "God is with you in all that you do." (Genesis 21:22 LITV) Everyone else was probably thinking the same thing. The covenant Abimelech wanted is stated in Genesis 21:23:

Now therefore swear unto me here by God that thou wilt not deal falsely with me, nor with my son, nor with my son's son: but according to the kindness that I have done unto thee, thou shalt do unto me, and to the land wherein thou hast sojourned.

One of the discoveries in ancient Gerar was a well. Water was an issue in Gerar, especially between Abraham's and later Isaac's herdsman and the Philistines. After coming to an agreement concerning water rights, Abraham conducted the covenant ritual according to his rules of honoring God with seven ewe lambs. Abraham planted a tree as a reminder of the agreement and a testimony of God's goodness. The agreement was upheld by Abraham's descendants. It was the Philistines who eventually broke it when Isaac came to live there.

Genesis 21:1 should fill the hearts and minds of every believer until we grasp how dependable God's word is. "And the LORD visited Sarah as he had said, and the LORD did unto Sarah as he had spoken." Sarah knew for sure that nothing was impossible with God, nothing too hard for Him. As New Testament believers we can be confident like Sarah that "For as many promises as are of God, in Him they are yes, and in Him are Amen, for glory to God through us." (2Corinthians 1:20 LITV)

Sarah was one happy lady. "God hath made me to laugh, so that all that hear will laugh with me." (Genesis 21:6) She would live another thirty-seven years in joyful thanksgiving to a God who never abandoned her or her dreams. But first there was something she had to take care of.

Ishmael had grown into a young man. He was fourteen when Isaac was born. His situation didn't look as good as it had before. At best, he was a co-heir with this little brat everyone gushed over. After Isaac was weaned,

Abraham threw a big party. Everyone rejoiced with Abraham and Sarah over their miraculous son and enjoyed celebrating with the heir of Abraham's fortune. Really, who couldn't like a toddler named laughter?

For one Ishmael. For two Hagar. Let's start with Hagar. Before Isaac's birth, she may have been plotting to get rid of Sarah if Abraham died first. Who would stop her? Her son was the heir. After Isaac's birth, she probably did not appreciate her son being demoted to a secondary heir. Even though Ishmael was firstborn, concubine's sons either had to be adopted by the father or accepted by the legal wife. It docs not seem Sarah ever accepted Ishmael as her own.

Abraham on the other hand was fond of Ishmael. He had asked God to bless him. Certainly Abraham had plans to. He may have been planning to make him a co-heir, despite God's choosing of Isaac. Abraham could designate whatever Ishmael was to inherit of his own holdings such as livestock.

Hagar was confident Abraham loved Ishmael. She was right. But she underestimated Sarah's influence— again.

Ishmael was at least fifteen or sixteen by the time of the party. He may have been making plans of his own, dreaming of his inheritance. Was he stirred on by his mother to misbehave? Perhaps, but his character was not pleasant. God had said about him, "his hand will be against every man, and every man's hand against him." (Genesis 16:12) Strife followed him and his quarrelsome nature.

Sarah saw something that day. It was not just an older sibling teasing a toddler. It was darker, more menacing. Sandwiched between the story of Isaac and Ishmael in the New Testament Paul says, "But as then he that was born after the flesh persecuted him that was born after the Spirit..." (Galatians 4:29) Persecuted? Seems out of place between a sixteen year old and a two or three year old.

Ishmael was the one born of the flesh, the laws and customs according to man, the desire of Abraham. Isaac was the son of the promise, born by the power of God who is spirit. Ishmael's descendants would certainly persecute Isaac's, but there was an ominous nature about whatever Sarah witnessed at the party.

The word mock is *tsachaq* (sahKHAK), and it can mean to scorn or to laugh. It is the same word used in Exodus 32:6 when the people sinned against or mocked God, and in Judges 16:25 when the Philistines made fun of blind Samson. This was not harmless jesting. It may even have involved physical contact as in 2Samuel 2:14.

Sarah may have remembered her own humiliation under Hagar. The violence was *châmâs* (huhMAS). It's purpose was to demean and usurp. She may have recognized Hagar's control over Ishmael. God had not given Sarah a miraculous son to have his position threatened by rabble. God had sustained her through famine, Pharaoh, Hagar, Abraham, Abimelech and childlessness. He wasn't going to fail her in His promise to make Isaac the heir and a nation.

She boldly approached Abraham with the verdict: Hagar and Ishmael had to go. She wasn't going to accept Ishmael as an heir. But it was Abraham's decision to cast out or to free a slave woman's son. "Cast out this bondwoman and her son." (Genesis 21:10) Cast out is *gârash*, divorce. Sarah wanted it clear to everyone; Isaac was the only heir.

Abraham balked at first. Exceedingly spoiled by breaking to pieces are the words used to describe his emotions. Sarah demanded the separation of father and son, and it was breaking Abraham's heart.

Breaking the clump was the term used to sever family ties with the intent of disinheriting an heir.[10] Abraham did love Ishmael. But

---

[10] Dr. Robert Paulissian, "Adoption in Ancient Assyria and Babylonia," *Journal of Assyrian Academic Studies* Volume 13 No. 2 (1999) pg 24.

breaking the clump was legal if the son was found to be disrespectful or making claims against another heir. He and Sarah might have argued. Abraham decided to consult God. Surely this would put an end to Sarah's wrath and fear for Isaac.

But God told him to do what Sarah said. The threat may have been real. The fact was Ishmael had no inheritance rights in Canaan. It was all Isaac's. For Abraham, the time had come to fess up to the consequence of his choices. He had misjudged the offer of taking Hagar. He had heard God say Ishmael was not the heir. His mistake had become a crisis.

But it wasn't Ishmael's fault. God did not judge him. He told Abraham, "the son of the bondwoman will I make a nation, because he is thy seed." Legally, the disinherited received no property and had no right to. The father was to give some compensation. God took that responsibility on Himself. Ishmael would be taken care of.

Abraham always obeyed quickly. The following morning he sent Ishmael and Hagar away. They must have been shocked. Their only going away gift was bread and water. Later in his life, after Sarah died, Abraham had other sons. Those he sent away with gifts. Ishmael received nothing at his departure. At least his mother was free.

Divorcing Hagar and abandoning Ishmael was harsh. But God did not forget His promise to bless Ishmael. He heard the boy's voice when Ishmael had given up. "And God heard the voice of the lad; and the angel of God called to Hagar out of heaven, and said unto her, What aileth thee, Hagar? fear not; for God hath heard the voice of the lad where he is. Arise, lift up the lad, and hold him in thine hand." (Genesis 21:17-18)

Hold him in the hand refers to support; literally it may be read make your hand strong on him. Weak, disillusioned, struggling with rejection, the teenager needed encouragement. God gave it to him.

There are similarities between this part of Ishmael's story and the Binding of Isaac. For instance, Hagar, at the moment she has surrendered her son to death, looks up to discover the means of their deliverance. "And God opened her eyes, and she saw a well of water; and she went, and filled the bottle with water, and gave the lad drink." (Genesis 21:19)

The Bible says Ishmael grew into a great nation. Hagar got him an Egyptian wife. Perhaps no other type would do for her. Whether she ever considered God again or not, He kept His promise. Ishmael had twelve sons and lived to be 137.

We are never told what happened to Hagar. It is possible she had more family because there are references to Hagarites listed separately from the Ishmaelites. But they lived near each other. The tribe of Reuben took over their land. The Bible states they were enemies of Israel and by the time the prophets talk about them it was to pronounce curses on them.

Somewhere along the way, Ishmael himself gave up persecuting Isaac. He may have thought his life turned out better. Isaac had only two sons, Jacob and Esau. Only one of them, Jacob, followed Isaac's ways. When Esau realized his parents weren't pleased with the decisions he had made, he tried to amend his ways so he married Ishmael's daughter, Basemath. You can imagine how that went over.

While Isaac and Jacob still lived as strangers in Canaan, Ishmael was a prince and his sons rulers in their own land. The son of the flesh was materially blessed. Hagar must have been proud, indeed.

*A*braham couldn't watch as Hagar led Ishmael away. It wasn't the hatred in her dark eyes that weakened him. Truthfully, he did not mourn her leaving. Women like her survived. She, like a leopard on the borders of the Negev.

No it was Ishmael. The confusion clouding his eyes. The hurt in his sagging shoulders.

Tears ran down Abraham's cheeks as he walked toward camp. He sat on a rock and wept. What had he done? He never meant to hurt anyone. Regret. Remorse. Words he wished could cleanse them all from this tragedy.

Canaan held trying times for him. But not quite like the last years. It was a constant storm. He had shaken a nest of hornets and threw it in his tent. But he couldn't dodge the inevitable...

"Forgive me, Yhôvâh."

"Abba?"

Abraham wiped his face with his robe. "Here I am, Isaac. Does your mother know you came to look for me?"

The youngster jumped into his lap. "Eliezer sent me." He patted Abraham's beard. "I go to pastures today."

"You must stay close. Cattle are bigger than sheep, you know this?"

Isaac nodded, his eyes serious. Then he smiled. Abraham laughed. The boy was good. Not a cross bone ever. Abraham glanced at the path leading to the road. How very different he was than Ishmael. Ishmael needed to be handled. Isaac could be enjoyed.

Isaac pumped Abraham's arm. "Ready, Abba? Rest over?" He slid to the ground.

Abraham stood. He took Isaac's hand. "No Isaac. Yhôvâh has said it has just begun."

Chapter 8
The Binding of Isaac

Mt. Moriah may be the most important place on earth. It is the location of the Foundation Stone which Jews believe to be the site of the Holy of Holies of the First Temple. They also believe it is where God created Adam. It was where Melchizedek ruled as King of Salem and High Priest of the Most High God.

But the site lay quiet for years until King David bought the land, a threshing floor, from the former Jebusite king Araunah. (1 Chronicles 21:19-29 and 2 Samuel 24.) David needed it to stop a plague he had caused by disobeying God. Over that threshing floor the First Temple was built and finished in 957 BC. Archaeology has proven Mt. Moriah, the site of the Temple Mount, to be the location of the First and Second Temples.

Christians revere the Temple Mount for the same reasons as the Jews, since Christianity came from Judaism. But Christians add the New Testament to the Jewish Tanakh[1]. For Christians it is where Jesus was dedicated as a baby and where He sat with the priests when he was twelve years old. Jesus prayed and taught on Mt. Moriah many times,

---
[1] The Hebrew Bible contains the Torah (the first five books or Teaching), the Nevi'im (the Prophets) and the Ketuvim (the Writings). It is the Christian's Old Testament.

and it was the place where Jewish Christians began to meet after Jesus' resurrection.

Muslims call Mt. Moriah al-Haram al-Sharif, The Noble Sanctuary. They have claimed the Temple Mount for Islam and built the Dome of the Rock on it after they captured Jerusalem. The Dome of the Rock is a shrine sitting over what Muslims believe to be the spot where Muhammad visited the Jewish temple and met Abraham, Moses and Jesus. The Dome of the Rock is considered the most recognizable Jerusalem landmark. It is not a mosque, but there are five mosques on the Temple Mount.

You might have noticed by now Mt. Moriah is where Jerusalem is. Moriah sits with the Mount of Olives to the east and Mt. Zion to the west. It is important real estate for what are called the three Abrahamic faiths, Judaism, Christianity and Islam. Even though some Jews are not fond of Christians sharing their roots and adding Jesus to them, the stranger bedfellow is Islam.

After Hagar and Ishmael were sent away, Abraham had another encounter with God. This time God asked Abraham to sacrifice Isaac on Mt. Moriah. But Muslims say Abraham sacrificed Ishmael. They are the only ones to declare that as the Bible, the Jewish texts and the Dead Sea Scrolls say otherwise.

And their theory that Muhammad made his trip to heaven from the Temple? The First Temple was destroyed around 587 BC. The Second Temple was destroyed in 70 AD, and Muhammad wasn't born until five hundred years later in 570 AD.

Just to be thorough, Constantine's Christian Church of the Holy Sepulcher in Jerusalem was built in 335 AD and burned in 614 AD, seven years before Muhammad's supposed journey. But the church was not built on the Temple Mount. Therefore, no temple of any kind stood there or near it. Interestingly enough, the earliest traditions indicated Mecca for Muhammad's journey. It wasn't until the Umayyad caliphate (661-750) that the location became Jerusalem.

Today the "farthest mosque" quote in the Hadiths and Quran (which referred to the Jewish Temple) is translated as the Al-Aqsa Mosque. The problem with that idea is the mosque wasn't built until 705 AD, seventy three years after Muhammad died. You might think they meant Muhammad's spirit went on the journey. But the descriptions insist it was a physical and a spiritual journey. Other Muslims are interpreting the journey as a dream.

When an earthquake damaged the Al-Aqsa Mosque in 1927, British archaeologist Robert Hamilton photographed the mosque's damage and subterranean passageways. His pictures show evidence of Solomon's Temple. These photographs and sketches are kept by the Library of Congress and some are featured on the Israel Antiquities Authority website.

In 2016 and 2017 UNESCO, the special cultural arm of the United Nations, declared there was no Jewish connection to the Temple Mount. This was puzzling since the Muslims state the connection themselves through Muhammad's journey. And, the Arch of Titus in Rome still stands to contradict the claim.[2] It seems anti-intellectual to deny the obvious relics of the First and Second Jewish Temples. Jerusalem and the surrounding area is saturated with ancient Hebrew history.

In 2016, during UNESCO's announcement, *The New York Times* ran an article about an archaeological discovery they thought may have been timed by God.[3] The find was a papyrus fragment of a shipping receipt dat-

---

[2] The structure depicts the spoils of the Temple being brought back to Rome after Jerusalem was destroyed.

[3] Isabel Kershner, "As U.N. Ignores Jewish Ties to Holy Site, Israel Produces Ancient Evidence," *The New York Times*, October 26, 2016.

ing to the seventh century BC which had been analyzed, translated and prepared for publication. It contained the oldest mention of Jerusalem outside of the Bible written in ancient Hebrew, not Arabic. The fragment was a government correspondence between the king's maidservant for an order of wine from Na'arat to Jerusalem, the capital of Judah.

It may seem humorous that archaeology outwitted UNESCO and added its two cents to the Middle East conflict over Israel. But few people understand the ones to benefit from UNESCO's claims are only remotely related to Hagar's and Keturah's sons, the descendants of Ishmael and his six step-brothers.

While the strife appears to boil down to a step-family's discontent over Abraham's will, the real truth is Ishmael may be their rallying cry but not their DNA. Arabs are a mix of peoples—like everyone else—including Shem's sons like Joktan, and Japeth's sons and Ham's like Mizraim, the Egyptian. Even Esau is in the mix.

Fewer still acknowledge God's decree in the matter. He wanted Isaac to inherit Canaan and the blessing. We do not know if Ishmael was bitter about his treatment. But by the time God talked to Abraham about sacrificing Isaac, Ishmael was roaming the desert, becoming really good with a bow and arrow. (Genesis 21:20) Mt. Moriah was the last thing on his mind.

The incident known as the Binding of Isaac, The *Akedah*, is a much misunderstood story. It is found in Genesis 22 and begins like this:

> And it happened after these things, testing Abraham, God said to him, Abraham! And he said, Behold me. And He said, Now take your son, Isaac, your only one whom you love, and go into the land of Moriah. And there offer him for a burnt offering on one of the mountains which I will say to you.

> And Abraham started up early in the morning and saddled his ass, and he took two of his youths with him, and his son Isaac. And he split wood for a burnt offering, and rose up and went to the place which God had said to him. And on the third day Abraham lifted up his eyes and saw the place from a distance. (LITV)

Critics and skeptics point to this account and accuse God of cruelty. We agree that the event is meant to startle us. How could a good God require the killing of a young boy as an offering to Him? Wasn't God judging the Canaanites and taking their land from them for child sacrifice— among other things?

But as Christians we see it in the context God meant it: as a visual example of what He planned to do through Jesus, His only son. Notice that God called Isaac Abraham's only son. This is important because Isaac was not Abraham's only natural son. But he was the only son of the promise with a miraculous birth.

The idea of a triune God, Father, Son and Holy Spirit was not known to believers of Old Testament days. It was hidden in scripture, but not understood until Jesus came and introduced people to the Father and the Spirit, calling Himself the Son. Because it was not part of their traditional theology, the Pharisees in Jesus' day rejected the concept, looking instead for an earthly Messiah.

Sin, on the other hand, was something ancient man understood. They naturally assumed gods became angry at human behavior. They depended on sacrifices to appease gods. Human sacrifice was not uncommon, and it was thought pagan gods thrived on the smell of burnt offerings. Hazy and distorted in most cultures was a sliver of truth from Abel's sacrifices and the notion that blood paid for sins.

Today many rabbis reject the idea of Jesus dying to remove our sins because God never condoned human sacrifice. But others see that the animal provided by God was a substitute for Isaac. Modern Jewish thought considers the idea that Satan may have been behind Abraham's testing like he was for Job's.

The secular view is that it was only a story told to teach Abraham God did not accept human sacrifices, even one as highly regarded as an only son. The moral lesson was to teach future Israelites to conduct themselves differently than the pagan cultures around them who practiced human sacrifice.

Abraham may not have understood the full impact or meaning of his "testing" upon later generations, but he knew God was up to something. The word translated test or tempt is *nacah* (nahSAH). Test is the better translation into English because the Bible is clear God does not tempt us. (James 1:13) Isaac was never in danger.

But an even better word to describe God's purpose is prove. *Nacah* in English can mean test, assay, prove, try and adventure. It is used in Exodus 15:25-26. Against the standard of obedience to God, the Israelites would prove themselves. That is the pattern of "testing" from God. We either obey Him or we don't. The consequences are up to us.

Assay is an interesting word used to explain how metals are tested to show their quality. We take tests to prove the quality of our knowledge or skill. For example, a driving test proves to authorities our driving skills and our ability to own a license to drive.

Temptation arises from evil desires within us while a test comes from pressure applied through outside circumstances. Satan uses both to pressure us to disobey God and give up. When we are tried, what we believe spills out of our hearts and mouth, proving us. It can be victory or defeat; it depends on us and what we know about God.

Nacah also carries the meaning of being tried before a court. Abraham may have felt like that the morning he arose after his encounter with God. He was about to give his testimony of what was in his heart. He had time to mull over God's words on the forty to fifty mile trip to Mt. Moriah. One thing he did not surrender was his conviction that God was good.

We have no proof Sarah knew about God's conversation with Abraham. He told none of his servants. Not even Isaac. We do not know Isaac's age either. Scholars and rabbis debate ages from adolescence to mid to late thirties. This is contrary to the traditional, probably erroneous, picture of an elementary aged Isaac vulnerable to his father's wishes. That is the pagans' sacrificial template.

However old, Isaac was old enough to carry a generous supply of firewood up a mountain. Which brings us to the visual picture of Jesus and His journey to the cross.

There are similarities between the binding of Isaac and the crucifixion because God planned it that way. It is the only alternative that makes sense. Examine the parallels below:

- It was a three day journey from Beersheba to Moriah and both Isaac and Jesus were alive after three days.
- Abraham was pondering death and loss for three days like Jesus' followers,
- Isaac carried wood on his shoulder up a mountain like Jesus carried His cross to Golgotha.
- Moriah is in Jerusalem.
- Abraham walked with Isaac as God the Father was with Jesus.
- In both instances it was the loving father offering their miraculous, only sons of promise.
- Abraham carried fire, a symbol of the Holy Spirit.
- Abraham believed Isaac would be raised from the dead.

This startling image of a father sacrificing his son was seared into the minds of Hebrews. It was to be the lesson of the cross. Sadly many of those who entertained Jesus in their midst missed seeing its truth until He rose from the dead and told them. Many more people of all nations miss its importance today, choosing to focus instead on child sacrifice and God's supposed evil character. But God never intended for Isaac to be killed.

Abraham had left his two servants at the base of Moriah to wait. He said, "I and the lad will go yonder and worship, and come again to you." (Genesis 22:5) That was a remarkable statement because if Isaac ended up dead, Abraham had some explaining to do.

But Abraham received another revelation along with his instructions to take Isaac to Mt. Moriah. At some point, Abraham became convinced God could raise the dead. Remember when the Lord visited Abraham before He went to Sodom and asked, "Shall I tell Abraham that thing I do?" God revealed something to Abraham to give him the idea of resurrection.

Hebrews 11:17-19 says Abraham was reasoning "that God was able to raise him up, even from the dead." What would make Abraham conclude this? In John 8:56 Jesus tells us Abraham saw something. "Your father Abraham leaped for joy that he should see My day, and he saw, and rejoiced." (LITV)

The word translated saw is *eidō* (EYEdoh). It means to behold, to see, understand, perceive, be aware of and to know. At some point, Abraham got a revelation of Jesus as the Messiah and the resurrection.

But Abraham had already witnessed God raising a dead womb and an old man to life. If God could do that, He could raise the son whom He had provided. God gave the promise of one son to Abraham. There was no other accepted heir. The promise's fulfillment rested in him.

The Binding of Isaac

God had spoken repeatedly that He had given the land of Canaan to Abraham and that He had made him into a mighty nation. He also said the heir was going to be born to Sarah, and beyond all hope and expectation in a physical sense, the son was born. It had been a miracle and had happened exactly as God said it would. Isaac was the heir.

These words had gotten down into Abraham. They echoed in his head. He meditated the meaning of them in light of God's new command. He had learned God was good, that He rewarded trust and He was true to His word. These were the convictions behind Abraham's words to his servants. He may not have known how exactly, but Isaac was still the heir and the first of a nation. And God was about to do what He had never done before: He was going to raise the dead.

Abraham may have been surprised at God's command. The words spoken to him may have brought fear if he let his mind wander. He had given up one son, the son of his disobedience. This one he was giving up in order to be obedient. No wonder he didn't tell anyone about his mission. They would have thought he was crazy.

Not telling was the wisest thing he could do. People would have either fed his fear or told him a hundred and one reasons why he shouldn't obey the command. But Abraham was not the man he had been when he set foot in Canaan. His faith had been strengthened. He had come to know the God who spoke to him, appeared to him and delivered him from enemies, even when those enemies were the thoughts in his own mind. Somehow Abraham was certain God was working, something strange maybe, but something good.

To Isaac, who was wondering where the lamb was, Abraham said, "My son, God will provide himself a lamb for a burnt offering." (Genesis 22:8) We must be amazed at Isaac's willingness to become a sacrificial offering. The ancient historian Josephus says Isaac was twenty-five and dashed to the altar to be the victim.[4] That's a little hard to imagine don't you think?

Even so, Isaac never ran back down the mountain and whipped a donkey into a run to carry him back to his doting, sane mother. In fact, he said nothing as far as we know. He was still as he was bound and prepared for sacrifice. Indeed, Isaac was a picture of a willing Jesus, lying down, offering his limbs to Roman soldiers to place hands and feet on a cross and nail them there.

We can know Isaac was willing because it is also hard to imagine an old man winning a wrestling match with a healthy young boy who didn't want to be tied up and stabbed. No servants came running to answer his cries for help either. We might conclude there were no cries.

This was both Isaac's and Abraham's shining moment. Both passed the test of obedience down to the last minute. Both proved their devotion and their faith in a God who could raise the dead.

But God didn't want to give away His secrets just yet. The New Testament states if Satan had understood God was going to raise Jesus from the dead, he would have never killed Jesus. Isn't it amazing no one understood with all the prophecies God gave them? Satan didn't understand the Binding of Isaac at all.

Abraham never wrote down his vision or understanding of the Messiah and the resurrection. He just described the events as they unfolded. Like any good writer, he showed us instead of telling us. No one would fully understand the lesson until Jesus rose from the dead. The way had been prepared for making the connection through Isaac. Can you imagine Abraham and Isaac's reaction when Jesus showed up in Sheol? The day they looked forward to had come.

---

[4] Robin M. Jenson, "The Binding or Sacrifice of Isaac," *Bible History Daily*, Biblical Archaeological Society, September 7, 2018.

The male sheep in the thicket was God's provision, the Lamb He intended to provide all along since Genesis 1, and the Deliverer He spoke of in Genesis 3. We need to realize God provided for everything in those six days of creation. Hebrews 4:3 is one place the Bible tells us God finished His work and rested. His spiritual laws and things He purposed have been in motion since the foundation of the world. He did not have to scramble to come up with Plan B, C, and D after Adam and Lucifer screwed things up. The Lamb was already provided.

During his excavations in Ur, Iraq in 1928, Leonard C. Woolley found a sculpture he called Ram in a Thicket. The body and thicket were gold while the ram's ears were copper and its fleece was shell and lapis lazuli. The statue was an image of a goat and was one of two found in the Death Pits. Scholars believe the goat depicted in the statue is not caught but eating the leaves of the thicket, a common sight in the area even in modern times. Woolley named it Ram in a Thicket after Abraham's ram that was caught among the bushes of Mt. Moriah.

This misidentification is used to prove Abraham's story a myth. But just because this golden ram's horns are not entangled in the statues' tree does not prove there was no ram on Mt. Moriah. On the contrary. It proves the possibility of a ram becoming caught in the branches of a thicket by his horns as he browsed for his meal. Buckthorn, *Rhamnus lycioides,* or *Rhamnus palaestinus,* is one common shrub in Israel that grows in the Judean hills.

The thicket may also be symbolic of the cross. Scholars understand the thicket in a variety of applications. It could have been a symbol of the sin put on Jesus at his death. Some teach it was a representation of Jesus appointment to become the Savior and therefore bound Him in an agreement with God. Or, it was an image of the crown of thorns Jesus would wear at His death.

Where Abraham's ram came from and why Abraham or Isaac didn't see it before is a mystery. Abraham had said God would provide one Himself, and He did. The word for ram is *'ayil*. Its root word is *el* which is God or god. According to the *Ancient Hebrew Lexicon of the Bible* by Jeff A. Benner, it means strong one.[5] In his *Biblical Hebrew E-Magazine*, he defines it literally as "one that stands tall in might."[6] This was a perfectly strong male in its prime. Even the ram was a picture of Jesus.

Rosh Hashanah is one of the feasts celebrated in Jerusalem. The Binding of Isaac is retold during the second day of Rosh Hashanah. The ram's horn, a symbol of the one caught in the thicket, is blown as a reminder of how Isaac was spared. The Temple lies buried beneath the soil as the horn sounds over the hills of Jerusalem. Someday scholars believe Rosh Hashanah will be fulfilled at Jesus' Second Coming when the Lord will be seen.

Abraham named the place *Jehovahjireh* which translators have defined in English as the Lord will provide. Hebrew scholars translate it as the Lord will see or the Lord will be seen. Moriah means seen of Jah (the Lord). The location of Abraham's *Jehovahjireh* was remembered for over a thousand years. Both of its meanings are fitting for us today.

It was no coincidence this was the same place God told David to build an altar and offer sacrifices for his sins. David paid full price for the threshing floor like Abraham and Isaac gave their full trust. It was also no coincidence this was the site for the Temple. Genesis 22:14 calls it the mountain of the Lord, just so we remember who really owns it.

How long Abraham or Isaac kept the story of their experiences on Mt. Moriah a secret is uncertain. If Sarah hadn't known about it,

---

[5] Strong's H352.

[6] Jeff A. Benner, *Biblical Hebrew E-Magazine*, Issue #050, May 2009, Ancient Hebrew Research Center.

wouldn't you have liked to hear Abraham explain his actions to Sarah? However we might expect Sarah to respond, it was certain both were solid in their trust of God at this point in their lives.

Jewish tradition insists Sarah knew about Abraham's test and the proposed sacrifice of Isaac. Most of these scholars believe Isaac was an adult in his thirties. The strain of his near death caused Sarah's health to fail, they say, and she died soon after.

The Bible never says outright if Sarah knew or if she did not. It seems by the text that their life slowed down. Abraham settled in Beersheba. It must have been while he was living in Beersheba he received news of his brother's family.

> And it happened after these things it was told to Abraham, saying, Behold! Milcah, she also, has borne sons to your brother Nahor: Uz, his firstborn, Buz, and his brother Kemuel, the father of Aram, and Chesed, and Hazo, and Pildash, and Jidlaph, and Bethuel. And Bethuel fathered Rebekah. Milcah bore these eight to Nahor, the brother of Abraham. And his concubine, whose name was Reumah, she also bore Tebah, and Gaham, and Thahash, and Maachah. (Genesis 22:20-24)

Nahor had twelve sons, the same as Ishmael. Not all of Nahor's sons became nations, but there are a few men of interest on the list. The two oldest, Uz and Buz, are connected to Job. It may be hard to believe, but Uz and Buz may have been popular names.

The land of Uz was where Job lived. It was beyond the Euphrates according to one of the Dead Sea Scrolls called the War Scroll.[7] Another

---

[7] War Scrolls Column 2 Line 11 Qumran.org.

location for Uz is in southern Israel stretching to southwest Jordan.[8]

Buz is also mentioned in Job as an ancestor of Elihu. We've already talked about Chesed. Bethuel would become Isaac's father-in-law, and Maachah may have founded a small kingdom mentioned in Deuteronomy 3:14 and elsewhere.

Sarah died while at Hebron. Notice that Abraham did not mourn "his wife." He mourned for Sarah. For half her life she walked with him through Canaan. She had obeyed his requests and stood with him in his calling. They both had made mistakes, and they both had laughed together.

We know nothing of Sarah's background. But we can know something of her personality. In Isaac we see traces of Sarah. Isaac was the quiet, stable patriarch. His life embodied loyalty and obedience. His tenderness toward his wife was exactly opposite what we read of Abraham. Genesis 24:67 states "he loved her." The verse is more insightful when we realize Abraham or Isaac wrote those words. Abraham wasn't the only man to witness Isaac's love for his wife. In Genesis 26 Abimelech did too. Isaac's empathy can also be seen for Rebekah in her barrenness. He prayed *for her*.

To be fair, Abraham may have been the strong, silent type, the John Wayne of the patriarchs. Some scholars think Abraham had taken Keturah as his concubine while Sarah was living. They doubt he could have had more children after Isaac. But that is only opinion. Remember, no one thought he could have kids before Isaac either. Scholars also believe if he married Keturah after Sarah's death, her children would have been too young to send away before he died.

The argument about Keturah's sons being too young to send away is not a strong one. If Abraham married Keturah three years after

---

[8] This is perhaps the best location for Job's Uz since one of his friends, Eliphaz, was related to Esau who lived in the same region.

Sarah died, he would have been married to her thirty-five years. He sent Ishmael away when he was around sixteen. Keturah's sons were older than that and old enough to be on their own.

Some scholars object to Abraham taking Keturah after Sarah died because they say the story may not be chronological. But the events were in order as they happened up to the part about Keturah, weren't they? Do they fit another way? Archaeology showed evidence for Chedorlaomer's attack on Sodom before Sodom was destroyed. He couldn't have attacked it if it didn't exist. Nothing in Abraham's life story could be rearranged and make sense. This argument is not strong either.

Also, the idea of Abraham taking a concubine while Sarah was living conflicts with his past behavior. Genesis 25:1 is clear he is the one who "added," *yâsaph*. "And Abraham added and took a wife." (LITV) Added may simply mean along with Isaac's wife Rebekah, three years after Sarah's death.

Abraham had never taken another wife on his own. He deferred to Sarah's wishes as she had deferred to his. They were a team, sometimes for better, sometimes for worse. That was about as romantic as Abraham's story got.

Apparently Sarah and Abraham had returned to Hebron at some point after their settling in Beersheba, perhaps as part of the shepherding cycle. But Abraham may not have been with her at her death.

The reason for their separation is pondered by scholars and rabbis. Two of the most common answers have to do with the flock rotation from Hebron to Beersheba. She either went ahead of Abraham to Hebron or they were already in Hebron and she became sick. Then, when it was time to return to Beersheba, she stayed behind. The Bible says he went "in" to mourn. It may just mean he came in from the pastures or it may mean he had to travel from Beersheba.

Abraham bought a cave for Sarah's burial site from a Hethite named Ephron. Today it is called the Cave of the Patriarchs or the Cave of Machpelah. It is said Abraham took possession of it using the four methods of owning property. The four methods were 1) buying it, 2) through witnesses, 3) getting a deed, and 4) possessing it.

Abraham purchased the cave in a detailed exchange similar to real estate dealings in the Mari, Ras Shamra and Nuzi texts.[9] Phrases like full price, weighed out, give to you/give to me are found in Ancient Near Eastern deeds. Also included were the name of the owner, the type of property, its description, the price paid, the witnesses and the location of the property.

Some see in the dialogue a reluctance to sell Abraham, a foreigner by his admission, land. Others think Ephron took advantage of Abraham's need and made him purchase the field too so he could get more money. That made Abraham the owner who had to pay taxes.

We'd like to think Abraham respected Sarah so much he wanted to give her a prominent burial site. Actually rabbis think there was another reason. Abraham knew from his conversation with God and their first covenant that his descendants would be slaves in another country. It wouldn't be until they returned that they would take over Canaan.

Rabbis think Abraham wanted his descendants to have a place of connection to their past, a place they could claim as their ancestors'. So he bought the cave and surrounding field. Compared to what David had to pay for the threshing floor, Abraham had to pay far more than full price.

Abraham and Sarah were buried at Machpelah as well as Isaac and Rebekah and Jacob and Leah. Jews have always honored the site. Herod built a tomb over it which still stands today, 2,000 years after it was built.

---

[9] Gene M. Tucker, "The Legal Background of Genesis 23," *Journal of Biblical Literature* 85, no. 1 (1966): 77-84.

But by 1260 Muslim Mamelukes took over, and Jews and Christians were banned from visiting the tomb. In 1967 while the Jews had possession of Hebron, the Israeli people were able to visit the site for the first time in 700 years. Later, the Palestinians were given control of the cave.

In 2017, *Breaking Israel News* ran a story about Noam Arnon's secret adventure to find the cave. Arnon is a member of the Jewish community living in Hebron. Thirty-five years ago Jews were only allowed inside the tomb a few days out of the year because Muslims controlled the site. During the loud prayers of Selichot, Arnon and his friends waited for Arab guards to leave then pried up the stone door of the cave hidden by Arab prayer rugs. Descending stairs, they entered a room and searched for the cave.

Machpelah means doubled. What Arnon found was not one cave but two. They retrieved pieces of clay pottery dating to the First Temple. Later the head of the Israel Antiquities Authority investigated and dated the burial site to the Early Bronze Age.

But when Muslim residents found out about Arnon's escapade, they rioted. Muslim authorities cried foul, and the cave opening was sealed with concrete. Today Jews are allowed to access about one quarter of the tomb. No archaeological digs are allowed, and the UN has declared the Cave of the Patriarchs a Muslim holy site.

It is significant that the tomb holds three couples, the mothers and fathers of Israel. Sarah was the only woman in the Bible whose age was given at various times of her life. It was a mark of honor. 1 Peter 3:6 says if you are a believer, you are Sarah's child.

Years passed, and Isaac mourned his mother. This is another clue to the relationship he had with Sarah. He may have been closer to his mother than his father. Abraham called in his servant, probably the one he thought would be his heir, and established a verbal will. His priority? That Isaac not leave Canaan under any circumstances. And, Isaac needed a wife. The longest narrative in Abraham's story is about this servant's trip back to Aram-Naharaim.

Some rabbis interpret the servant's questions as proof the servant thought Abraham's request was unusual. A family member was the normal person to choose a wife for a son. Various scholars think Abraham's age was the reason Abraham did not go himself, and it is true that could have been a factor. But Hebrews 11:15 says Abraham did not even consider returning to his homeland.

Sending a servant to pick a wife was not that unusual. There is evidence of kings using servants to arrange marriages in the Amarna Letters. In EA 31, for example, is the negotiation of marriage between an Egyptian king and a Hittite king through a messenger named IrSappa. Professor Jack Sasson wrote about kings at Mari using messengers. Since Abraham acted like a king before, it doesn't matter if the extra-biblical evidence of servants arranging marriages only involves kings.

The servant's questions pointed out a woman may not have wanted to deal with a servant. To Abraham that was a deal breaker. If she demanded Isaac go there, forget it and come home, was Abraham's reply.

Then in a ceremony that seems odd to us, Abraham and the servant finalized their agreement with an oath of loyalty. Abraham told the servant to put his hand under the soft part of Abraham's thigh.

Dr. David Elgavish of Bar-Ilan University quotes Rabbi Shlomo Yitzchak (1040-1105) and Rabbi Nissim Ben Reuben Gerondi (1320-1380 AD) to explain why. Abraham was reminding his servant of the covenant of circumcision. It made Abraham and every one of his male descendants different. According to the rabbis, this oath was also a demonstration that no Hebrew was to marry a foreigner. Other commentators think the vow was about protecting Abraham's lineage.

When the servant returned with Nahor's beautiful granddaughter, Rebekah, Isaac fell in love. He took her to Sarah's tent, and their household was established. He and Rebekah lived mostly around Beersheba and near Hagar's well, Beer-lahai-roi.

We learned in earlier chapters that they moved to Gerar during a famine and that God would not let Isaac go down to Egypt. "And Jehovah appeared unto him, and said, Go not down into Egypt; dwell in the land which I shall tell thee of: sojourn in this land, and I will be with thee, and will bless thee; for unto thee, and unto thy seed, I will give all these lands, and I will establish the oath which I sware unto Abraham thy father." (Genesis 26:2-3)

Isaac obeyed, even though the famine was severe. Abimelech was the king in Gerar; either the same one Abraham knew or one of his sons. If you remember, Abimelech may have been a title.

Isaac became afraid for his life in Gerar too. He also had a beautiful, rich wife. He decided to lie, and use Abraham's ruse, declaring Rebekah was his sister. Only she was his second cousin, not a half sister. His deception really was a lie. Isaac may not have planned it out like his father, but when men began asking and he felt threatened by their interest, his father's deception looked pretty good.

Critics claim this account is a copy of Abraham's situation in Genesis 20. But there are too many differences for that to be true. For instance, Rebekah was never taken, and Isaac didn't gain any wealth from Abimelech when he found out the truth. He did get the king's protection. But God's favor was better. Isaac planted fields during that famine, and he harvested a hundred times as much as he planted. Even the Philistines admitted Isaac was blessed.

Rebekah, like Sarah, did not have children. For twenty years she was barren. Isaac prayed and God answered with twin sons, Jacob and Esau.

But Isaac's life was rather dull compared to his father's. He never battled kings. He never left Canaan. He never changed his name; perhaps because God named him. He never had concubines. Isaac's job was to continue gaining wealth, maintain a presence in Canaan and have a son to continue the promise. His twelve grandsons would become the twelve tribes of Israel.

His life was mostly peaceful, until his sons grew up and started fighting over their rights. But all that peace must have been good for him. Isaac was the longest lived patriarch. He died at 180.

He and Abraham had a long time to enjoy their work, their family and each other's company. One day, Abraham remarried. His priority had been Isaac. After Isaac married Rebekah, Abraham may have felt lonely. Keturah was called Abraham's wife and his concubine. She never held the status of Sarah, and she was listed with Hagar as a concubine. The distinction between a secondary wife and a concubine was not made until the period of the kings in Israel. Therefore, the Bible is not contradicting itself when it calls Keturah a wife and a concubine.

Abraham was around 140 years old when he added Keturah as his concubine. He must have still been exercising his faith because he had six more sons. These sons became nations in Arabia. Near the end of his life, the Bible says he gave gifts to them and Ishmael. "But unto the sons of the concubines, which Abraham had, Abraham gave gifts, and sent them away from Isaac his son, while he yet lived, eastward, unto the east country." (Genesis 25:6)

While he yet lived may be indicating they were younger than usual for sending away. Not as young as Ishmael as we have said, but younger than the average age for marrying. That age was thirty to forty.

Abraham's concubines were Hagar and Keturah. One of his sons Midian was the father of the Midianites. Midian was located in modern day northwest Saudi Arabia. Abraham's grandsons, Sheba and Dedan, are also associated with territories inside Saudi Arabia.

Ishmael's lands were east of the Dead Sea, beyond the ill fated cities of the plain. When Abraham died, Ishmael was there with Isaac to bury him in the Cave of Machpelah. Isaac's sons were fifteen. We do not know if they accompanied their father to Machpelah.

Isaac wrote the details of Abraham's death. He filled in the history of Ishmael and his sons. He began his own *towlĕdah* in Genesis 25:19, but he kept his father's carefully. So carefully Moses could use it to write Genesis.

Abraham's other sons are not mentioned. Maybe they were too far to the east and south, beyond Ishmael's lands, to hear of Abraham's death. Or, Isaac didn't bother to mention them. Keturah is not mentioned either. She may have been part of Abraham's household servants before she was a concubine. Perhaps she stayed to care for Abraham, or she may have left with her sons so that they could care for her as she grew old. We have no details how Abraham provided for her or even if she was alive when he died.

Abraham's history takes up fourteen chapters in Genesis. It is only a portion of one book in the Bible. But upon this man and his story, the rest of the Bible is built.

Indeed, an entire nation and the faith that can change lives began with one man's acceptance of an invitation and the dream of being a father.

*A*braham sat at the door of his tent, the stand of trees opposite. There under those trees, he thought. "Where is your wife?" the LORD had asked.

He gripped his staff. He should walk down to the flock. Later, he decided. Isaac would know to move them off the sun drenched hill to the wadi.

As if in answer little Esau ran across the slope and a line of sheep threaded down the hillside. Minutes later Isaac followed. He looked up and waved.

Abraham waved back. Isaac's smile warmed him, and he laughed again. He was a good boy, the son he had hoped for. "Thank you," he whispered.

Sarah would be proud of him, he thought. He was. Abraham felt the nearness of Macphelah. Isaac wanted to return to Beersheba, to settle. He was right. It was too crowded here. Isaac preferred the Negev. As well he should, since he had been raised there. Abraham liked it too. He named it had he not?

The wind rustled the leaves of the trees. But he had many good memories here...

"Saba."

Abraham turned on his stool as little Ya'ăqôb pressed a bowl of porridge into his hand. "Ah what have we here? My supper so early?"

"Eema thought you might be hungry,."

Abraham sipped the broth. "You take good care of me my son."

The lad knelt on the ground beside him. "Tell me about the visitors again. Those trees?" He pointed. "Yehovah sat under them?"

Abraham searched the boy's face. *What is this earnestness I see in his eyes, Yhôvâh? What are You about in the heart of one so young?*

He leaned his staff against the post. In the distance Esau trotted back up the hillside, disappearing among the rocks with a stick in his hand.

Little Ya'ăqôb's hand rested on his knee. Abraham smiled at him. Isaac used to sit at his feet. He grasped Ya'ăqôb's thin hand in his and something stirred inside him. Abraham chuckled. So it is this one you have chosen is it, Yhôvâh?

"Oh blessed Ya'ăqôb," he said. "I will tell it all to you."

From Abraham to the Twelve Tribes of Israel

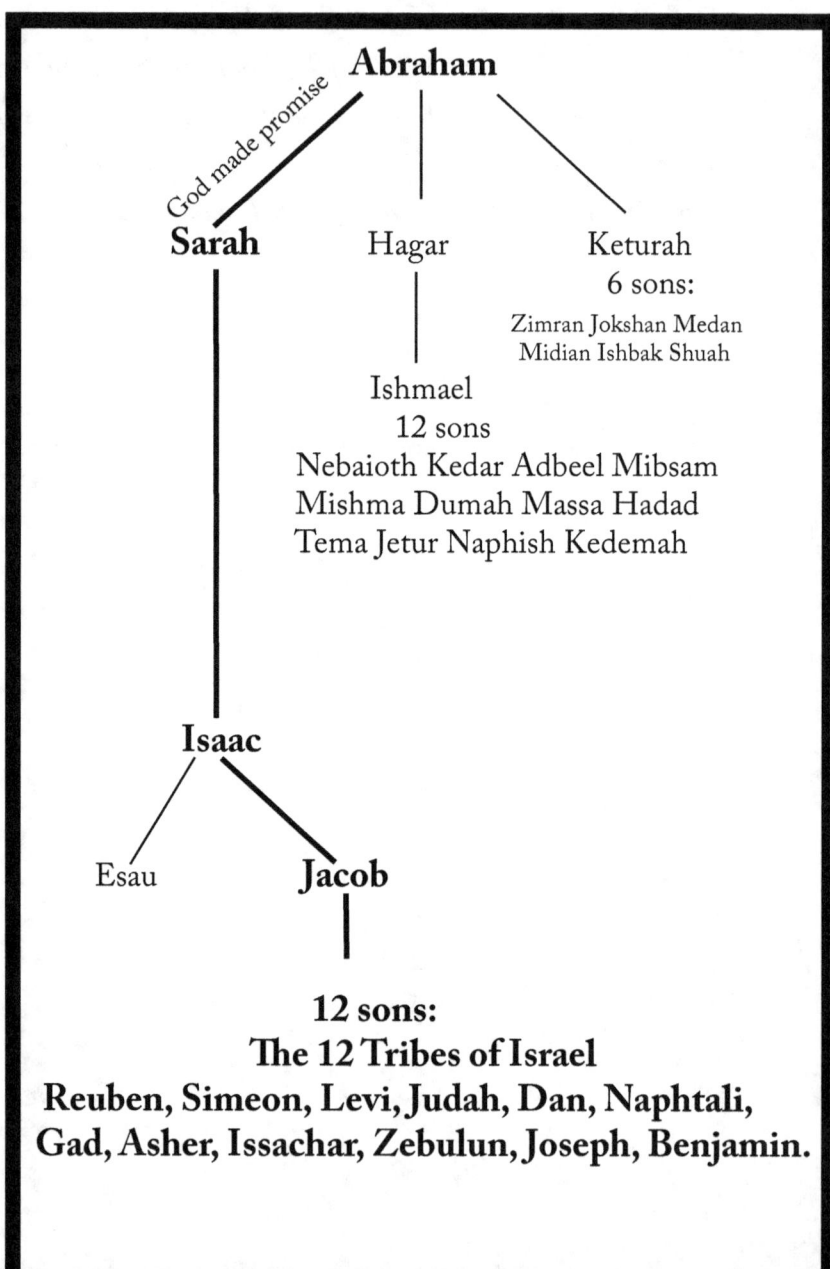

Chapter 9
Abraham's Legacy

Abraham died at the age of 175. He had spent 100 of those years in Canaan. It may not have seemed like much at the time, but his obedience set off a series of miracles that created a nation. It was a chain of events fueled by Abraham's undying conviction to take God at His word.

It was quite an accomplishment for a man who never gave his name to anything. His father and grandfathers had towns named for them. But of Abram or Abraham we have no monuments, no statutes. Instead he left altars. There may be one exception inscribed on a list of towns taken by Pharaoh Shishak I. Among the cities of the Negev appears *pa'ha-q-ru-a 'i-bi-ra-ma*, the fortifications of Abram.[1] Perhaps a family member assigned his name to the region.

In Galatians 3:7 Abraham is called the father of all who have faith in Jesus as Lord. All, Hebrew and non-Hebrew. Galatians 3:28-29 is the great equalizer of God's kingdom. "There is neither Jew nor Greek, there is neither bond nor free, there is neither male nor female: for ye are all one in Christ Jesus. And if ye be Christ's, then are ye Abraham's seed, and heirs according to the promise."

[1] P. Kyle MCCarter "Abraham as a Historical Figure" My Jewish Learning.

God never qualifies us by our flesh identity. Like Abraham we are made right by what we believe, specifically by our belief in Jesus. Romans 4:16-17 says, "Therefore it is of faith, that it might be by grace; to the end the promise might be sure to all the seed; not to that only which is of the law, but to that also which is of the faith of Abraham; who is the father of us all, As it is written, I have made thee a father of many nations."

Abraham may be dismissed for the moment by many in the world who do not accept him as a historical person with an extraordinary life. But one day his children will be revealed. Believers of every tongue and nation, we are his monuments.

For a man who is so ridiculed by historians, however, he pacts punch in the political landscape of the Middle East. Abraham is believed by Muslims to be the first man to submit to Allah. But Abraham himself would say that isn't so. He said his God was Yahweh. We mispronounce the Hebrew and say Jehovah, but this God whom Abraham worshipped and built altars to has a very different character than Allah. In Quran 3:95 Allah advises his followers to follow the religion of Abraham which ironically was not Islam.

It is not well received when it is said Muslims have to change Abraham's *towlĕdah* to practice their religion. They say he built the Kaaba in Saudi Arabia and went there to worship. But unless Muslims are willing to say Saudi Arabia was part of Canaan and therefore Israel's, Abraham left Canaan once to go to Egypt. He never left again. Alternative stories are also created for Ishmael, Jacob, Joseph, Moses and Jesus among others in an attempt to Islamicize them.

And that slave girl from Egypt? Her hamas spirit lives in the root of every contention between Muslim and Jew or Christian. The drive to displace, disinherit and minimize can be traced to a young Egyptian mother. The fights can be traced to two brothers with Jewish heritage, one with a warring, jealous heart and an eye to prove his superiority.

But Abraham loved Ishmael, Isaac and his six sons, and he loved Jesus more. He personally made every effort to be fair to each son, and God fulfilled those desires. Today, God stands waiting to embrace their descendants in love, along with anyone else who would choose Him the way Abraham did.

But Islam is not the only Abrahamic faith to morph Abraham into something he was not or to add to his story. There are many variations of Jewish background stories in the Midrash for Abraham and Sarah that go beyond what was written in Genesis. None of these can be verified.

God told Abraham that all the nations on earth would be blessed through him. Jesus fulfilled that prophecy. Galatians 3:7 says Abraham is "the father of all who believe." But many so-called believers overlook the facts. Abraham had a relationship with Jesus and called Him Lord. While Islam denies Jesus is God and demotes Him to a prophet beneath Muhammad, Judaism rejects Jesus or only marginally accepts Him as a teacher.

One modern Jewish doctor tells of the time he asked his rabbi about the possibility of having a relationship with God. The rabbi pulled his umbrella from under his arm and hit the doctor over the head. "Blasphemy!" he cried.[2]

Jesus is a bad word in many Jewish homes because they have been taught the New Testament is a Gentile book that teaches people to hate Jews. Most don't think they need Jesus because they are descended from Abraham; they are Jews and Jews don't need Jesus. And, none want to stop being Jewish and accept Jesus.

---

[2] Dr. Miller, "A Jewish Doctor finds cure for the soul," One For Israel Ministry, YouTube December 24, 2018.

That is why ministries like Jews for Jesus and One For Israel are considered cults. According to Christian Jews Eitan Bar and Moti Vaknin, one rabbi threatened to murder them.[3] The Israelis even debate if Christian Jews may return to Israel under what is called the Right of Return or *aliya,* the act of going up toward Jerusalem. *The Jerusalem Post* quoted one official saying, "If someone declares that they believe in Jesus, then he is not a Jew... A Jew who wants to immigrate to Israel will move to Israel if he can prove his Judaism."[4] Of course other officials are willing to recognize Jewish ancestry even if they might disagree about Jesus.

But many Jews are surprised when they read the New Testament to find a Jewish Jesus, a grandson of Abraham, and a Jewish culture threaded throughout the books. The Jewishness is what ministers to them. They understand the message of the circumcision of the heart, the covenant and the Binding of Isaac better than most Christians. Despite being labeled a cult, there are about 30,000 Christian Jews in Israel.

Christianity is also guilty of stretching Abraham. It over reaches to fit the needs of evolution, or minimizes his message for a social gospel and to serve liberal theology. That is, for those who even believe Abraham was a real person and not a bedtime story. For example, there are sincere Christians who date Genesis much later and even into the tenth century BC.

Abraham is touted by many religious teachers to be the poster child for senior citizens. He was old when he was called. Therefore, God uses old people. Of course he does. But not many want to have children when they are ninety or a hundred. Abraham didn't either.

---

[3] Famous Israeli Rabbi publicly entices to MURDER two Israeli Messianic Jewish evangelists, One For Israel, YouTube, October 21, 2015.

[4] Tamara Zieve, "Will Israel Ever Accept Messianic Jews?" *The Jerusalem Post*, December 16, 2017.

He had hoped he would have had family by then. But leaving Harran when he was seventy-five, Abraham was not even middle aged. He spent more than one of our lifetimes as a foreigner in Canaan.

He entered Canaan the equivalent of a man in his thirties or forties, according to his lifespan. Did he look like a forty year old? We don't know. His body may have been aging faster than his father's. But the deeper lessons of Abraham's life, such as nothing is impossible to those who believe, apply to persons of any age.

Other theologians declare Abraham was man's last chance to have a relationship with God. To say that, they ignore the Priest and King Melchizedek who worshipped the Most High God. He probably wasn't the sole believer in Jerusalem. In IKings 19, Elijah was convinced he was the last man standing. But there were other believers he knew nothing about. There were probably others in Abraham's day we know nothing about.

One of the great privileges in our day is the birth of archaeology and its role in uncovering the cultures of the past. But what has archaeology taught us about Abraham?

While either Ur may have been where Abraham was living, his home was in northern Mesopotamia in modern Syria near the Turkey border, a region rich in archaeological treasures. Abraham, we now understand, dates to the period called the Early Bronze Age 1 and the Early Dynasty period in Egypt. Cities were thriving and civilizations were spreading farther and farther. Trade routes were well established; schools taught foreign languages and advanced math.

The Bible tells us Abraham's life overlapped with Shem's. Arphaxad, Shelah and Eber were also living. It is possible Abraham heard Shem's account of the true God and the pre-flood world. Noah died only a few years before Abraham was born. Statues, temples, homes and factories have been uncovered that show us the world the ancients lived in. It is a world that continues to surprise evolutionists.

The setting and cultural practices revealed in Abraham's account are supported by ancient texts and discoveries at Ebla, Mari, Nuzi, Ugarit, Ur and other sites in northern Mesopotamia. Ancient Hebrew words and phrasing can also be found among these sources. Excavations at Shechem, ancient Bethel, Hebron, Dan, En Gedi, Sodom and Gomorrah support his story as well.

Discovered sources even suggest his war against five kings was not invented and inserted later in history. The story was told by an eyewitness and written down by a writer who knew ancient Hebrew (pre-Babylonian Hebrew) and Egyptian. The real truth is the Bible introduced us to the Early Bronze Age through Abraham before we ever knew there was an Early Bronze Age. It showed us an ancient language which has survived to the present day with a few variations. It named towns no one would have known existed and told us where to look for them.

More could be listed here about what archaeology has found supporting Abraham, but you've read this far; you know. If such strong evidence points to the truth of Abraham's life story as told in the Bible, a story that existed before archaeology existed to prove it authentic and one that introduced us to a world that was before unknown, what does it suggest about the rest of his story, his journey to confident trust in God?

The odds are it is all true and worth investigating. Abraham never set out from Harran to create a religion...or three. He just wrote down his conversations with God and what he did and what happened. We are left to study his life and wonder what it means for us today. And when we wonder, wherever we are, whoever we are, God is able to make Himself known to us. What we do with God depends on us. Like Abraham, we choose by obedience or disobedience to God's word.

For those who have already received God and believe Abraham's story is true, what does Abraham teach us, his children, about faith?

God requires complete and total trust. The *Amplified Bible* (Colossians 1:4) defines faith as a complete leaning of one's personality on God. This is what Abraham modeled for us when he left Harran for Canaan. He made the decision not to look back. Hebrews 11:15 says that if Abraham and Sarah had rehearsed the memory (*mnēmoneuō*) of the country they left, they might have thought to return. But neither considered it or allowed it to tempt them.

The complete leaning was a process in other areas of their lives, however. For instance Abraham, like us, had to find those areas in himself that were influenced by the world around him. Sometimes we don't even know that how we behave, react or think is not God's method for living. Abraham showed us his struggle to rid himself of his culture's influence and operate only by God's methods.

His path to success came when God spoke to him, he understood what to do and he believed God would do what He said in every area of his life. We have God's word in the Bible to lead us, hundreds of examples there to teach us, and we have our conversations with God. We also have the indwelling Holy Spirit to give us wisdom and revelation.

Total obedience is crucial. Abraham was obedient to what he knew to do. We read Abraham's missteps. We read his questions. We see God's kindness and mercy toward him. We even see God's corrective rebuke, but with the purpose of love as His goal. We learn then that obedience moves us forward and shields us in mercy.

Abraham had to set out from Harran, and God met Him when He arrived in the right spot. Abraham's journey wasn't over. His one hundred years in Canaan had just begun. But he had to start walking, and God met him on the way. We just have to believe, just start walking in obedience to what we know, and God supports our efforts. The trip wasn't even for Abraham especially. It was for all people, those he would never meet while on earth. Abraham's life teaches us that obedience and disobedience to God results in a chain reaction that affects others.

One thing Abraham teaches us is to ask questions. We discover he would have been better off he would have asked even more. We can ask God for wisdom and direction, yes, but how about asking what to pray about, how to talk to Him, what questions to ask Him and even the everyday things like what to wear, what to eat and which way to drive to work or school? It is important to cultivate a state of mindfulness and surrender to God instead of cutting a rut of habitual reactions in our daily life. Lean not on our own understanding Proverbs 3:5 says. This is one way to avoid proceeding by our flawed reasonings.

Abraham had to receive what God had already done for him, such as giving him land, making him into a nation, making him rich in a foreign country. On his own, Abraham could accomplish none of these things on the scale God wanted to give him. Making him into a nation implied he had a son already. Only, Sarah was barren. Abraham learned God spoke of things as though they already were. Jesus did the same thing in John 17:4 when He said His work was finished. He hadn't been crucified yet.

When Jesus tells us in Mark 11:24 that we need to believe we have what we ask for in prayer, He is expecting us to think and act like we already have it, past tense. It is the way He spoke to Abraham and therefore the way He thought. He advises us to do the same if we want answers. It seems too bold, aggressive perhaps. But realizing we aren't fighting God for it, that He wants to say yes to whatever He has promised— health, provision, salvation, love, etc.— is the biggest stumbling block to belief. It is how Abraham had to look at his situation.

It wasn't just for fun that God have Abram a new name. For Abram to fulfill his destiny and the dream God had put in his heart for a son, he needed to see himself differently. Abram had to put on his new identity so he became Abraham in his heart. It wasn't the lie of mind over matter. It was the powerful creative force of God's word over matter which brings us to the next point.

Abraham had to learn a higher law controlled and commanded the physical world. The physical world may be fact at the moment but it is not the reality. He knew Sarah's body had experienced menopause. All hope for children was removed.

Abraham had to admit Sarah was beyond having children. He saw that he was old, his body as good as dead. But he put his hope in words spoken to him anyway because what he could see as fact could change.

The lesson is the world hidden to our eyes is more real than circumstances. Reality came in the form of words spoken by the Creator of life itself. Jesus said His words are life and they are spirit. God's word is alive, and when we speak it, the physical world listens. Abraham had to understand this was a law and it could work for him. All he had to do was believe. Here is what the New Testament says about Abraham:

> Who against hope believed in hope, that he might become the father of many nations, according to that which was spoken, So shall thy seed be. And being not weak in faith, he considered not his own body now dead, when he was about an hundred years old, neither yet the deadness of Sara's womb: He staggered not at the promise of God through unbelief; but was strong in faith, giving glory to God; And being fully persuaded that, what he had promised, he was able also to perform. And there-

fore it was imputed to him for righteousness.
Romans 4:18-22

Abraham had to choose the authority speaking into his life. We all listen to words and repeat them. We don't always realize their source or their power. When he listened to the words playing in his head about adopting his servant he wasn't listening to God. He was regurgitating the world's methods into his life. He did the same thing when he listened to Sarah.

But twenty-four years after leaving Harran, Abraham learned not to live by his sight or his circumstances. The verse says he wouldn't even think about his body or Sarah's. So what did he consider? Only God's promise, ability and goodness.

As we've learned, God's methods are different than the world's. You may wonder why since God created the world. But God created the world to operate as Eden operated. When Adam and Eve used their free will to sin, they didn't know they were passing the authority God had given them to Satan. Satan became the ruler of earth only because God remained faithful to His decision to give Adam dominion. But tied to Adam's obedience was God's blessing. The blessing was removed when Adam disobeyed. It is called the fall of man. He was demoted, not by God, but by his own hand and Satan's cunning.

But in Abraham we see God moving to reenact the blessing through faith in Him and obedience to His word. Abraham saw Jesus. He believed His words and through this kind of faith, Abraham became righteous or made right.

Abraham wasn't perfect. He sinned. He made mistakes. But he believed in Jesus before the law was given to Moses. This is what Paul, a Jewish Pharisee inspired by the Holy Spirit, wanted to make plain when he wrote Romans 4:16. "Therefore it is of faith, that it might be by grace; to the end the promise might be sure to all the seed." James, another Jew, wrote in James 2:23 "Abraham believed God, and it was imputed unto him for righteousness: and he was called the Friend of God." Imputed means assigned. He didn't earn righteousness; it was given to him because he believed in Jesus.

The Bible assures us these things weren't written for Abraham's sake alone but for ours. "Now it was not written for his sake alone, that it was imputed to him; But for us also, to whom it shall be imputed, if we believe on him that raised up Jesus our Lord from the dead; Who was delivered for our offences, and was raised again for our justification." (Rom 4:23-25)

Abraham had to continue to stick with God. If we choose God as the Authority speaking into our lives, then we are back to remaining in a place of complete trust in Him. God doesn't like uncertainty about His loyalty, His love or His ability. He doesn't like it because it hinders His ability to work in us.

James 1:6-8 calls it being double-minded, unstable and wavering. "But let him ask in faith, nothing wavering. For he that wavereth is like a wave of the sea driven with the wind and tossed. For let not that man think that he shall receive any thing of the Lord. A double minded man is unstable in all his ways."

God requires us to be all in, not looking back, not fearful because fear is doubt. Peter could walk on water until he turned his eye away from Jesus. When Abraham looked at his childlessness, it spoke back to him. Failure. Hopelessness. Loss. He had to remain in one place like Jesus tells us in John 15:7. "If you remain in Me, and My Words remain in you, whatever you desire you will ask, and it shall happen to you." (LITV) Sarah had to discipline her fear thoughts and attitudes too. Hebrews 11:11 says she received God's power to conceive.

When the circumstances speak to us, we need to cast them on the Lord. It is our job to remain. It is His job to supply. Abraham and Sarah had to learn this lesson, and it took them a while to get it right.

You might wonder if all the trusting and believing is of any value to us today. Testimonies abound that prove it is. Maren Hamm from Wisconsin found out that taking God at His word held the healing no doctor had been able to provide. She was diagnosed at nine years old with various diseases and had symptoms no medical procedure relieved.

In 2015, when she heard the same message that Abraham heard and did the same thing Abraham had done, she was totally healed. And there are others who tell a similar story.[5] Those who were bipolar, legally blind, had cancer, lupus, an aneurysm, muscle pain, heart problems, hearing loss and yes, even the dead raised to life. Pastors and teachers like Kenneth Hagin, Greg Mohr, Duane Munoz, Todd White and Andrew Wommack have experienced it themselves and are telling others like those before them such as F.F. Bosworth and Smith Wigglesworth.

Abraham also has taught us a few things about covenants. We've learned they are forever binding. We also discovered the people involved in the covenant become one blood and therefore family. They were assured protection and provision. Abraham had a covenant that passed to all believers. But a Christian circumcision is one of the heart like it says in Deuteronomy 30:6.

We also learned we are heirs to Abraham's covenant of blessing with God through our faith in Jesus. (Galatians 3:29) Hebrews 8:6 tells us Jesus has given us a better covenant established on better promises. The old covenant guaranteed earthly blessings, and the new adds eternal life in the presence of God.

---

[5] Links to Maren's testimony and others can be found in the Bibliography under Healing Testimonies.

Many theologians stress the heavenly blessings that await us and drop the earthly part of Abraham's blessing. But Galatians 3:13-14 clearly includes the earthly blessing as well. "Christ redeemed us from the curse of the Law, having become a curse for us; for it has been written, 'Cursed is everyone having been hung on a tree;' that the blessing of Abraham might be to the nations in Christ Jesus, that we might receive the promise of the Spirit through faith."

Jesus is the mediator of this new covenant, and His blood, Hebrews 12:24 says, speaks a better word, meaning it completes our need of forgiveness because it is superior to any other sacrifice. All we need to do is receive what has already been done for us, just like Abraham. The Bible says we have been given everything for life and godliness. The abundant life is what Jesus has made possible for us now while we live on the earth in the same way He took care of Abraham while he walked in Canaan.

Abraham's biggest feat and lasting fame came to him just by daring to believe the word of God. It changed his life and has benefited men and women from every generation, from every tribe and tongue.

The legacy of Abraham goes beyond the conflicts in the Middle East. It can be seen in every night time prayer of little children said in Jesus' name. The faith of those praying for the poor and over the sick. The hope of every interceding believer on behalf of those in danger. In the praise and proclamation at every altar in synagogue or church. One day Abraham's legacy will be seen on Mt. Moriah as a ram's horn sounds.

Despite the clamor among his physical children, Abraham is the great uniter of our hearts. Believers anywhere can look to Abraham and to Sarah, the rock from which they are cut.

Abraham teaches us faith and faithfulness. He teaches us to look up when circumstances pull us down. And he teaches us to believe when everyone says it's impossible. He even teaches us to believe when the world says his life is only myth, his story unimportant, because he knows if we search we will find the Truth. Just like he did back in Ur of the Chaldees.

If you have never asked Jesus into your heart, start here.

Abraham was confronted with the existence of the One God, Creator and Most High. He made the decision to partner with Him and allow Him to be the boss over every area of his life. Abraham's promise has been fulfilled and is still being fulfilled as people trust in God as Abraham did in Ur.

You see, Jesus, the promised Seed, has completed His work of salvation, and it is an open invitation to anyone who wants it. He chose to come into this world to do what we couldn't, start over and right our wrongs. We consistently do wrong. It's called sin, and unfortunately we are born into it because of the fall of man recorded in Genesis 3. We live our life with blinders on, never realizing it.

But Jesus gave us a way out of darkness. He came to earth, lived a perfect life and volunteered to take all our sin and the consequences we deserve upon Himself. He did it on the cross. And then, He rose from the dead, defeating sin and death.

Sure, everybody dies. But if you are in Jesus, He calls it sleep. Just like a little kid who falls asleep in the car and wakes up somewhere else, we'll wake up in heaven.

We can have victory by accepting Jesus' work as a gift. It is the way He made, the method He planned, even before the Binding of Isaac.

Jesus' gift is easy to receive. Just like Abram had to believe in God who was able to make him Abraham and had to confess the new reality of his identity, we receive by believing and confessing.

"… if you will confess with your mouth that Jesus is Lord, and believe in your heart that God raised him from the dead, you will be saved. For with the heart, one believes resulting in righteousness; and with the mouth confession is made resulting in salvation." (Rom 10:9-10 WEB)

If you would like to be born again into a new and different person on the inside, forgiven and washed clean, in partnership with the Creator of your life who is able to fulfill the purpose of the inmost desires of your heart, pray this prayer:

"Jesus I believe You are Lord; that You came and died on the cross and were raised from the dead. I believe that You died to save me, and I ask You to live Your life in me. Fill me with your Holy Spirit. Thank You for forgiving me. Thank You for loving me. Amen."

Pretty simple. But these words have power to change you. Just like Abraham. Now go and tell someone. Then go and tell someone else.

For more about faith, check out the blog at Flying Eagle Publications.

Thank you for your purchase of *From Abram to Abraham*. If you enjoyed the book, please leave your review online. Check out our website flyingeaglepublications.com for more and take a look at other books in this series.

Bibliography

Adamthwaite, Murray R. "A northern Sodom?" *Journal Of Creation* 30(1) 2016. pp 33-36.

Africa, Thomas W. "Herodotus and Diodorus on Egypt." *Journal of Near Eastern Studies* 22, no. 4 (1963): 254-58. http://www.jstor.org/stable/543808.

"A Jewish Doctor finds cure for the soul," YouTube Video, 5:27, posted by One For Israel Ministry, December 24,2018.https://www.youtube.com/watch?v=rEA0Y9xg43s

Aling, Charles PhD. and Clyde Billington PhD. "The Name Yahweh in Egyptian Hieroglyphic Texts." Associates For Biblical Research. March 08, 2010. http://www.biblearchaeology.org/post/2010/03/08/The-Name-Yahweh-in-Egyptian-Hieroglyphic-Texts.aspx

Ancient Sumerian References (2200 - 2000 B.C.E.) israel-a-history-of-.com. http://www.israel-a-history-of.com/ancient-sumerian.htm

Archi, Alfonso. *Lapis Lazuli and Shells from Mari to Ebla in Overturning Certainties in Near Eastern Archaeology,* Netherlands:Brill, 2017. https://doi.org/10.1163/9789004353572_004

Arnold, Bill T. and Bryan E. Beyer *Readings from the Ancient Near East: Primary Sources for Old Testament Study (Encountering Biblical Studies)* (Grand Rapids:Baker Academic, 2002).

Astour, Michael C. "Toponymy of Ebla and Ethnohistory of Northern Syria: A Preliminary Survey," *Journal of the American Oriental Society* 108, no. 4 (1988): 545-55. doi:10.2307/603144.

"Bab edh Dhra, Jordan with Dr. Randall Price," YouTube Video 2:20 posted by World of the Bible, July 27, 2018. https://www.youtube.

com/watch?v=KcNageF_dSs

Balint, Judy Lash. "The Bedouin in Israel." My Jewish Learning. 2019. https://www.myjewishlearning.com/article/the-bedouin-in-israel/

Balofsky, Ahuva. "Hebron: Controversial Archaeological Dig to Resume." *Breaking Israel News,* January 15, 2014.

Bar, Dr. Shaul. "Abraham's Trees," *Abraham IBS* Vol 28, Issue 1 2010. 2-20. https://biblicalstudies.org.uk/pdf/irish-biblical-studies/28-1_002.pdf

Bar-Am, Aviva and Shmuel. "How did Abraham get from Mesapotamia to the Promised Land?" *Times of Israel,* May 9, 2015. https://www.timesofisrael.com/how-did-abraham-get-from-mesapotamia-to-the-promised-land/

Barton, George A. "The Historical Value of the Patriarchal Narratives." Proceedings of the American Philosophical Society 52, no. 209 (1913): 184-200. http://www.jstor.org/stable/983865.

Benner, Jeff A. "Bless Barak." Ancient Hebrew Research Center. 2019. http://www.ancient-hebrew.org/vocabulary_definitions_bless.html
___ "The Archives of Ebla and the Bible." Ancient Hebrew Research Center. 2019. http://www.ancient-hebrew.org/bible_ebla.html
___ "The Goat Hair Tent of the Hebrew Nomads." Ancient Hebrew Research Center. 2019. http://www.ancient-hebrew.org/culture_tent.html
___ "The meaning of Grace from a Hebrew perspective." Ancient Hebrew Research Center. 2019. http://www.ancient-hebrew.org/articles_grace.html

Ben-Shlomo, David PhD. "The Ancient City of Hebron." The Torah.com https://thetorah.com/the-ancient-city-of-hebron/

Ben-Tor, Amon. "Do the Execration Texts Reflect an Accurate Picture of the Contemporary Settlement Map of Palestine?" The Hebrew University, Jerusalem. p 3. Academia. Accessed 2019. https://www.academia.edu/25340113/Do_the_Execration_Texts_Reflect_an_Accurate_Picture_of_the_Contemporary_Settlement_Map_of_Palestine

Berger, Yotam and Jack Khoury. "Israel Approves $6 Million Expansion of Hebron Jewish Settlement," *Haaretz*, Oct 14, 2018.

Berlin, Rebecca. "How Did Friends Impact American Culture?" Prezi. Updated June 28, 2015. https://prezi.com/lvqobxgll853/how-did-friends-impact-american-culture/

Berlyn, Patricia. "The Journey Of Terah:To U-Kasdim Or Urkesh?" *Jewish Bible Quarterly*. 33.2 (2005) 73-80.

Berman, Joshua. "Histories Twice Told: Deuteronomy 1—3 and the Hittite Treaty Prologue Tradition." *Journal of Biblical Literature*, 132, no. 2 (2013): 229-50. doi:10.2307/23488010. https://www.jstor.org/stable/23488010?read-now=1&seq=6#page_scan_tab_contents

Biblical Archaeology Society Staff. "Ancient World's Largest Cemetery Identified at Biblical Zoar (Ancient Zoora)," *Bible History Daily*, February 28, 2012.

Black, Emily, David J. Brayshaw, and Claire M. C. Rambeau. "Past, present and future precipitation in the Middle East: insights from models and observations." *Philosophical Transactions of the Royal Society A: Mathematical, Physical and Engineering Sciences*, Vol 368, Issue 1931, November 28, 2010. http://doi.org/10.1098/rsta.2010.0199

Black, J.A., Cunningham, G., Fluckiger-Hawker, E, Robson, E., and Zólyomi, G., The Electronic Text Corpus of Sumerian Literature (http://www-etcsl.orient.ox.ac.uk/), Oxford 1998- . http://etcsl.orinst.ox.ac.uk/section2/tr215.htm

Blech, Rabbi Benjamin. "Judaism & the Power of Names." Aish. April

20, 2013. http://www.aish.com/jw/s/Judaism--the-Power-of-Names.html

Boissoneault, Lorraine. "What Really Turned the Sahara Desert From a Green Oasis Into a Wasteland?" *Smithsonian.com,* March 24, 2017. https://www.smithsonianmag.com/science-nature/what-really-turned-sahara-desert-green-oasis-wasteland-180962668/

Borschel-Dan, Amanda, "4,000-year-old prenup pushes for surrogacy in case of infertility," *The Times of Israel,* November 12, 2017.

Bramwell, Ellen S. "Chapter 18 Personal Names and Anthropology," In *The Oxford Handbook of Names and Naming,* (Oxford:Oxford University Press, 2016) pp 18.1-18.3.

Bright, John. *A History of Israel,* (Westminster:John Knox Press, 2000). Google Books.

Buccellati, Giorgio and Marilyn Kelly-Buccellati. "In Search of Hurrian Urkesh City of Myth" *Odyssey,* May/June 2001. 16-27.

Byers, Gary. "The Jordan River Valley, the Jordan River and the Jungle of the Jordan." Associates For Biblical Research. June 6, 2007. https://biblearchaeology.org/research/patriarchal-era/3844-the-jordan-river-valley-the-jordan-river-and-the-jungle-of-the-jordan

Capart, Jean and A. S. Griffith Translator. *Primitive Art in Egypt* (London:H. Grevel & Co., 1905) Fig 179 p 240. NYU Digital Library. http://dlib.nyu.edu/awdl/sites/dl-pa.home.nyu.awdl/files/primitiveartin00capa/primitiveartin00capa.pdf

Casanova, Amanda. "Archaeologists May Have Found the Old Testament City of Ai." ChristianHeadlines. February 15, 2019 https://www.christianheadlines.com/blog/archaeologists-may-have-found-the-old-testament-city-of-ai.html

Cassius Dio, "Epitome of Book LXVI," *Roman History* Vol. VIII of the Loeb Classical Library edition, 1925. paragraphs 21-22. http://penelope.uchicago.edu/Thayer/E/Roman/Texts/Cassius_Dio/66*.html

Cendana, Kat. "Astronomy and Astrology." Amazing Bible Timeline with World History. March 10, 2016. https://amazingbibletimeline.com/blog/astronomy-and-astrology/

"Chaldea, Chaldeans." Encyclopaedia Judaica. Encyclopedia.com. (March 11, 2019). https://www.encyclopedia.com/religion/encyclopedias-almanacs-transcripts-and-maps/chaldea-chaldeans

Chivers, C. J. "Grave Robbers and War Steal Syria's History," *The New York Times,* April 6, 2013.

Clendenen, E. Ray. "Did Those Places Really Exist?" *Apologetics Study Bible* (Nashville, Tennessee :Holman Bible Publishers, 2007) 25.

Cooper, Ashley, Spelman Smith Fielding and others, "The Institution of Cyrus," in *The Whole Works of Xenophon* (London: Jones & Co 1832) 38-44. Google Books.
Cooper, M.A.Spelman, E. and Smith, W. and Fielding, S. and Welwood, J. and Graves, R. and Bradley, R. and Moyle, W. and Stanley, T. *The Whole Works of Xenophon* Classical library 1843 T. Wardel (Harvard University digitalized version 2007) also available on Amazon *The Whole Works Of Xenophon - Primary Source Edition* (Nabu Press, 2013).

Crawford, Harriet. *Ur: The City of the Moon God,* (London:Bloomsbury Academic, 2015).

Danzig, David. "Ebla and the Bible: A Case Study in Comparative Semitics and Literature," July, 25, 2010. Academia. http://www.academia.edu/827904/Ebla_and_the_Bible_A_Case_Study_in_Comparative_Semitics_and_Literature

Dio, Cassius. "Epitome of Book LXVI," *Roman History* Vol. VIII of the Loeb Classical Library edition, 1925. paragraphs 21-22. http://penelope.uchicago.edu/Thayer/E/Roman/Texts/Cassius_Dio/66*.html

Easton, M.G. "Chaldea," in *Easton's Bible Dictionary*, (New York:Scriptura Press, 1893) Esword.
Easton, M.G. "Euphrates," in *Easton's Bible Dictionary*, (New York:Scriptura Press, 1893) Esword.

Elgavish, David PhD. "Marital Customs as Reflected in the Account of the Marriage of Isaac and Rebekah." Parashat Chaye Sarah 5756, No. 106. Bar-Ilan University. https://www.biu.ac.il/JH/Parasha/eng/chaye/esarah2.html

Ellis, Maria DeJ. "An Old Babylonian Adoption Contract from Tell Harmal." *Journal of Cuneiform Studies,* 27, no. 3 (1975): 130-51. doi:10.2307/1359240.

Eusebius of Caesarea, *Onomasticon* (1971) Notes. pp. 76-252. Ed. C. Umhau Wolf. Christian Classics Ethereal Library. https://www.ccel.org/ccel/pearse/onomasticon.iii.html Accessed July 2, 2019.

"Famous Israeli Rabbi publicly entices to MURDER two Israeli Messianic Jewish evangelists," YouTube Video, 3:50 posted by One for Israel Ministry, October 21, 2015. https://www.youtube.com/watch?v=JLFz28ZhE_s

Fears, Darryl. "Fears The Sahara is growing, thanks in part to climate change," *The Washington Post,* March 29, 2018.

Fitzgerald, Madeleine André. "The Rulers of Larsa." Degree of Doctor of Philosophy. Graduate School of Yale University. May 2002. https://www.academia.edu/4370993/THE_RULERS_OF_LARSA

Flavius, Josephus. *The Jewish War* . Book 4 Chapter 8 Section 4 (4.8.4) By William Whiston, M.A. (London:Cambridge, 1737). http://penelope.uchicago.edu/josephus/war-4.html

Friedman, Saul S. *A History of the Middle East,* (Jefferson, North Carolina:McFarland & Co Inc, 2006). Google Books.

Garrard, A.N., N.P. Stanley Price with a contribution by L. Copeland. "A Survey of Prehistoric sites in the Azraq Basin, Eastern Jordan," *Paléorient,* Vol 3, 1975-1976-1977.p 109-126.

Gascoigne, Bamber. "History Of Astrology." History World. From 2001, ongoing. http://www.historyworld.net/wrldhis/PlainTextHistories.asp?historyid=ac32

Glassman, Ronald M. *The Origins of Democracy in Tribes, City-States and Nation-States (*Springer International Publishing, 2017) 464-465, Google Books.

Gordon, Cyrus H. "Abraham and the Merchants of Ura." *Journal of Near Eastern Studies* 17, no. 1 (1958): 28-31. http://www.jstor.org/stable/542500.
____ "Where Is Abraham's Ur?" *Biblical Archaeology Review* 3:2, June 1977.

Gornall, Jonathan. "When Arabia was green: lush grasslands helped early man make leap out of Africa," *The National UAE,* May 13, 2015. https://www.thenational.ae/uae/when-arabia-was-green-lush-grasslands-helped-early-man-make-leap-out-of-africa-1.114720

Grigg, Russell. "Meeting the ancestors," *Creation,* 25(2):13–15, March 2003.

Habermehl, Anne. "Where in the World Is the Tower of Babel?" *Answers Research Journal*, Vol.4, March 23, 2011, pp. 25-53.

HaCohen, Dr. David BenGad. "Abram at the Battle of the Kings: When Was the Dead Sea the Valley of Siddim?" TheTorah.com November 10, 2016. https://thetorah.com/abram-at-the-battle-of-the-kings-when-was-the-dead-sea-the-valley-of-siddim/

Hallen, A. "The Caphtorim. Who Were These People and Where Was Their Original Home?" *The Old Testament Student* 6, no. 8 (1887): 243-45. http://www.jstor.org/stable/3156981.

Hamilton, Victor P. "Abram Meets Two Kings (14:17–24)" *The Book of Genesis: Chapters* 1-17, (Grand Rapids:Eerdmans, 1990) 407-416.

Hansen, David G. "Shechem: Its Archaeological and Contextual Significance." Associates For Biblical Research, June 25, 2010. https://biblearchaeology.org/research/new-testament-era/2365-shechem-its-archaeological-and-contextual-significance?highlight=WyJzaGVjaGVt Iiwic2hlY2hlbSdzIiwic2hlY2hlbSciXQ==

Harms, William. "Evidence of battle at Hamoukar points to early urban development," *The University of Chicago Chronicle* , Vol. 26 No.8 Jan. 18, 2007. http://chronicle.uchicago.edu/070118/hamoukar.shtml
___ "Linking ancient peoples" *The University of Chicago Chronicle*, Feb. 1, 1996 Vol. 15, No. 10. http://chronicle.uchicago.edu/960201/hittites.shtml

Harris, Graham. *The Destruction of Sodom: A Scientific Commentary.* (Cambridge, UK:Lutterworth Press, 2015).

Harris, William E. *From Man to God: An LDS Scientist Views Creation, Progression and Exaltation (*Canada:Horizon Pub & Dist Inc., 1989) 52 -53. Harris cites *A Revelation in Archeology* (pg 10) and *The Archives of Ebla* (pg 249) as his sources.

Healing testimonies. https://www.awmi.net/video/series/healing-journeys/

Heide, Martin. *The Domestication of the Camel: Biological, Archaeologi-*

Bibliography

cal and Inscriptional Evidence from Mesopotamia, Egypt, Israel and Arabia, and Literary Evidence from the Hebrew Bible. Ugarit Forschungen. 42. 148-184. 2011. 10.13140/2.1.2090.8161.

Heimpel, Wolfgang. *Letters to the King of Mari: A New Translation, with Historical Introduction* (University Park, PA:Eisenbrauns, 2003), 26.

Hennerbichler, Ferdinand. Kar-da^{KI}-ka 21st ce. B.C.E. Karda Land of Valiant Mountain People Central Zagros East Terminological Analysis. Advances in Anthropology, (2014). 04. 168-198. https://doi.org/10.4236/aa.2014.43021.

Highnett, Katherine. "Biblical City Of Sodom Was Blasted To Smithereens By A Massive Asteroid Explosion," *Newsweek*. November 22, 2018.

History.com editors, "Palmyra." History. August 23, 2018. https://www.history.com/topics/ancient-middle-east/palmyra

Hodge, Bodie and Paul F. Taylor. "Doesn't the Bible Support Slavery?"*New Answers Book 3*. Online: Answers in Genesis. January 19, 2015. https://answersingenesis.org/bible-questions/doesnt-the-bible-support-slavery/
Hodge, Bodie. "Josephus and Genesis Chapter Ten A Wonderful Stepping-Stone," *Answers in Depth* Vol. 4 November 18, 2009.

Horne, Lee. "Ur and Its Treasures The Royal Tombs," *Expedition*, Online Penn Museum, Volume 40 Issue 2 1998.

Holst, Sanford. "Origin of the Phoenicians: Interactions in the Early Mediterranean Region," Queen Mary College, London, England, June 29, 2008. Phoenicians The Phoenician Experience. http://www.phoenician.org/origin_of_phoenicians.htm

"Israel The Land: Geography and Climate." Embassy of Israel New

Zealand. https://embassies.gov.il/wellington/AboutIsrael/Land/Pages/THE%20LAND-%20Geography%20and%20Climate.aspx

Jennings, James E. "The Problem Of The Caphtorim," *Grace Journal* University of Akron. 23-45. https://biblicalstudies.org.uk/pdf/grace-journal/12-2_23.pdf

Jewish Virtual Library, s.v. "Mari," accessed May 7, 2019. https://www.jewishvirtuallibrary.org/mari
____ s.v. "Tadmor," May 7, 2019. https://www.Jewishvirtuallibrary.org/tadmor

Johnston, Grahame. "The Early Bronze Age." Archaeology Expert. Sep 5, 2012. http://www.archaeologyexpert.co.uk/early-bronze-age.html

Jones, Clay. "The Horror of Canaanite Children's 'Family' Life." Clay Jones. April 27, 2015. https://www.clayjones.net/2015/04/canaanite-children/#footnote_8_1304

Kagan, Elsa Joy, Dafna Langgut, Elisabetta Boaretto, Frank Harald Neumann and Mordechai Stein. "Dead Sea Levels During The Bronze And Iron Ages," *Radiocarbon*, Vol 57, Nr 2, 2015, p 237–252 DOI: 10.2458/azu_rc.57.18560© 2015 by the Arizona Board of Regents on behalf of the University of Arizona https://journals.uair.arizona.edu/index.php/radiocarbon/article/view/18560/18208

Kennedy, T.M. "The Date of Camel Domestication in the Ancient Near East." Associates For Biblical Research. Feb 17, 2014. http://www.biblearchaeology.org/post/2014/02/17/The-Date-of-Camel-Domestication-in-the-Ancient-Near-East.aspx

Kershner, Isabel. "As U.N. Ignores Jewish Ties to Holy Site, Israel Produces Ancient Evidence," *The New York Times,* October 26, 2016.

"King Seal Artifacts Attest to Hebron's Jewish History." Hebron. 2019. http://en.hebron.org.il/history/693

Kitchen, K. A. "Chapter 3 Ebla Queen of Ancient Syria," In *The Bible in Its World: The Bible and Archaeology Today.* (Eugene, Oregon: Wipf and Stock Publishers, 2004) 37-55. Akkad Sargon's capitol has never been found p 48.

Kloosterman, Karin. "10 top ways Israel fights desertification." Israel 21c. July 15, 2012. https://www.israel21c.org/top-10-ways-israel-fights-desertification/

Kohn, Gabriel PhD. "Say You Are My Sister" Bar-Ilan University's Parashat Hashavua Study Center. Parashat Lekh Lekha 5765. October 23, 2004. https://www.biu.ac.il/JH/Parasha/eng/lekh/koh.html

Kordova, Shoshana. "Word of the Day / Hamas: The Terror Movement That Didn't Do Its Hebrew Homework," *Haaretz,* August 4, 2014. https://www.haaretz.com/word-of-the-day-hamas-1.5257987

Kramer, Joel. "The Oldest Yahweh Inscription." Associates For Biblical Research. Jan 20, 2017. http://www.biblearchaeology.org/post/2017/01/20/The-Oldest-Yahweh-Inscription.aspx

Krasnov, Boris and Emanuel Mazor. *The Makhteshim Country: A Laboratory of Nature : Geological and Ecological Studies in the Desert Region of Israel,* (Sofia, Bulgaria:Pensoft Publishers, 2001.)

"Labor And Slavery In Mesopotamia." Facts and Details. September 2018. http://factsanddetails.com/world/cat56/sub363/entry-6082.html

Larue, Gerald A. "Religious Traditions and Circumcision," The Second International Symposium on Circumcision, San Francisco, California, April 30-May 3, 1991. http://www.nocirc.org/symposia/second/larue.html

Lawler, Andrew. "City of Biblical Abraham Brimmed With Trade and

Riches," *National Geographic*, March 11, 2016.

____ "Who Were the Hurrians?"*Archaeology* Volume 61 Number 4, July/August 2008.

Leslau, Wolf. *Hebrew Cognates In Amharic,* (Wiesbaden: Otto Harrassowitz, 1969), 47.

"A Letter from Abdu-Heba of Jerusalem EA 286." Reshafim.org http://www.reshafim.org.il/ad/egypt/a-abdu-heba1.htm
"Letters by Rib-Addi of Byblos EA 75, EA 79, EA 122, EA 137 and others." http://www.reshafim.org.il/ad/egypt/a-rib-addi.htm

Limbert, John. "The Origins and Appearance of the Kurds in Pre-Islamic Iran." Iranian Studies 1, no. 2 (1968): 41-51. http://www.jstor.org/stable/4309997.

Living Passages. *A Holy Place: Eli Shukron Explains How the Melchizedek Standing Stone Was Kept Hidden*, You Tube, April 25, 2018 https://www.youtube.com/watch?v=_EKaN6FXwVw
____*Inside Temple Zero: Eli Shukron talks Melchizedek and the anointing of the House of God*, You Tube, April 30, 2018 https://www.youtube.com/watch?v=ry8UrMLnjjI

Mafalani, Haifaa. "Ebla, Tell Mardikh, Memory of the Orient," *The Syrian Times,* May 23, 2018.

McCarter, Kyle P. "Abraham As A Historical Figure." My Jewish Learning. https://www.myjewishlearning.com/article/abraham/

McClellan, Matt. "Abraham and the Chronology of Ancient Mesopotamia," *Answers Research Journal,* Vol. 5, October 3, 2012, pp141-150.

Megahed, Mohamed, and Hana Vymazalova. "Ancient Egyptian Royal Circumcision From The Pyramid Complex Of Djedkare." *Anthropologie,* (1962-) 49, no. 2 (2011): 155-64. http://www.jstor.org/

stable/26272374.

Millard, Alan R. "Where Was Abraham's Ur The Case for the Babylonian City" *Biblical Archaeology Review* 27:3, May/June 2001.

Moran, William L. *The Amttrna Letters*, EA 290, (Baltimore,Maryland:John Hopkins University Press, 1992) Full Text Amarna Letters, Internet Archive. 2019. https://archive.org/stream/TheAmarnaLetters/The%20Amarna%20Letters_djvu.txt

Morris, John D. PhD. "Have Sodom and Gomorrah Been Discovered?"Institute For Creation Research. March 29, 2013. https://www.icr.org/article/have-sodom-gomorrah-been-discovered

Na'aman, Nadav. "Habiru and Hebrews: The Transfer of a Social Term to the Literary Sphere." *Journal of Near Eastern Studies* 45, no. 4 (1986): 271-88. http://www.jstor.org/stable/544204.

Ngo, Robin. "Did the Carthaginians Really Practice Infant Sacrifice?" *Bible History Daily,* April 2, 2018. https://www.biblicalarchaeology.org/daily/ancient-cultures/did-the-carthaginians-really-practice-infant-sacrifice/

Nixon, Brian. "More Evidence Confirms Tall el-Hammam as Sodom," *Assist News Service.* August 21, 2018.

Notre Dame University. "Excavations @ Bab edh-Drah'." Bab edh-Drah Bioarchaeology. Accessed July 2, 2019. https://www3.nd.edu/~nsfbones/nsfbones/Dhra.html

Ortner, Donald J., and Bruno Frohlich. *The Early Bronze Age I Tombs and Burials of Bâb Edh-Dhrâ', Jordan.* Vol 3. (Lanham, MD:Altamira Press, 2008).

Osgood, Dr. A.J.M. "The Times of Abraham," *Journal of Creation* 2(1):77–87, April 1986. https://creation.com/the-times-of-abraham

O'Toole, Thomas. "Ebla Tablets: No Biblical Claims," *The Washington Post,* December 9, 1979.

Owen, Lewis, McGuire Gibson and Seton H.F. Lloyd. "Tigris-Euphrates river" in Encyclopaedia Britannica. https://www.britannica.com/place/Tigris-Euphrates-river-system#ref495876

Paulissian, Robert, PhD. "Adoption in Ancient Assyria and Babylonia," *Journal of Assyrian Academic Studies,* pp5-34. http://jaas.org/edocs/v13n2/Paulissia1.pdf

Pelgrift, Henry Curtis. "Mari Definition," Ancient History Encyclopedia. January 19, 2016. https://www.ancient.eu/mari/

Pettinato, Giovanni. "The Royal Archives of Tell Mardikh-Ebla," *The Biblical Archaeologist* Vol. 39, No. 2 (May, 1976), pp. 44-52

Pierce, Larry. "Chronology Wars." Answers in Genesis. January 01, 2010. Accessed March 26, 2019. https://answersingenesis.org/bible-history/chronology-wars/.

Pinches, T. G. *Journal of the Royal Asiatic Society of Great Britain and Ireland,* 1907, 738-40. http://www.jstor.org/stable/25210479.

Porat, Naomi, Uzi Avner, Assaf Holzer, Rahamim Shemtov, and Liora Kolska Horwitz. "Fourth-Millennium-BC 'Leopard Traps' from the Negev Desert (Israel)." *Antiquity* 87, no. 337 (2013): 714–27. doi:10.1017/S0003598X00049413.

Price, Campbell. "Texts in Translation #13: The Stela of Sobek-khu (Acc. no. 3306)." Egypt at the Manchester Museum. https://egypt-manchester.wordpress.com/2014/04/10/texts-in-translation-13-the-stela-of-sobek-khu-acc-no-3306/

Pryke, Louise M. "The Many Complaints to Pharaoh of Rib-Addi of

Byblos." *Journal of the American Oriental Society* 131, no. 3 (2011): 411-22. http://www.jstor.org/stable/41380709.

Rast, W., and R.T. Schaub, *Bâb edh-Dhrâ': Excavations at the Town Site (1975-1981)* (Eisenbrauns, 2003).

Resenberger, Boyce. "Ebla Ruins Shed Light on Early Urban Man," *New York Times,* January 16, 1979.

Reznick, Rabbi Leibel. "Biblical Archeology: Sodom and Gomorrah." Aish. Apr 5, 2008. http://www.aish.com/ci/sam/48931527.html

Rinat, Zafrir. "Disappearance of Elephants in Land of Israel May Have Led to Birth of Modern Man." *Haartz,* December 13, 2011.

Sanders, Charles L. PhD. *Did Jesus Believe Genesis?* (DeLand, FL:Holy Fire Publishing, 2012) 261 Googlebooks.com

Sasson, Jack. "Circumcision In The Ancient Near East," *Journal of Biblical Literature*, 85.4, 1966, Society of Biblical Literature, Vanderbilt University, pgs 473-476. https://ir.vanderbilt.edu/handle/1803/3895?show=full
Sasson, Jack M. "The Servant's Tale: How Rebekah Found a Spouse." Journal of Near Eastern Studies 65, no. 4 (2006): 241-65. doi:10.1086/511101.

Sauter, Megan. "Did Camels Exist in Biblical Times?" Biblical Archaeology Society. November 12, 2018. Accessed May 04, 2019. https://www.biblicalarchaeology.org/daily/ancient-cultures/ancient-near-eastern-world/did-camels-exist-in-biblical-times/.

Schreiner, Dr. David. "Pondering the Spade: Mari and the Mari Texts," Wesley Biblical Seminary. August 30, 2016. https://wbs.edu/2016/08/pondering-the-spade-mari/

"Slavery." Penn State. Accessed 2019. http://sites.psu.edu/ancientmesopotamianwarfare/slavery/

Smith Jr., Henry B. MA. "Genocide in Canaan? Part II." Associates For Biblical Research. Feb 06, 2013. http://www.biblearchaeology.org/post/2013/02/06/Genocide-in-Canaan-Part-II.aspx

Stone, Adam. "Nanna/Suen/Sin (god)," Ancient Mesopotamian Gods and Goddesses, Oracc and the UK Higher Education Academy, 2016 [http://oracc.museum.upenn.edu/amgg/listofdeities/nannasuen/]

Stripling, Scott and Mark Hassler, "Biblical City Of Ai Located." Patterns of Evidence. Feb.9, 2019. https://patternsofevidence.com/2019/02/09/biblical-city-ai-located/

"Tents in the Ancient World." Bible History Online. 2019. https://www.bible-history.com/links.php?cat=39&sub=425&cat_name=Manners+%26+Customs&subcat_name=Tents

"The Digital Dead Sea Scrolls." Israel Museum. 2019. http://dss.collections.imj.org.il/war

"The First Towns Early Bronze Age 3300 - 1950 BCE." University of Pennsylvania Museum of Archaeology and Anthropology. https://www.penn.museum/sites/canaan/EarlyBronzeAge.html

Thomas, Brian PhD. "Archaeology Confirms Genesis, Job Climate." Institue For Creation Research. September 20, 2016. https://www.icr.org/article/archaeology-confirms-genesis-job-climate/

Trumbull, Henry Clay. *The Blood Covenant: A Primitive Rite and Its Bearing on Scripture* (New York:Charles Scribner's Sons 1885). Google Books.

Trustees of the British Museum, "Domuztepe Excavation of a Late Neolithic settlement in south-central Turkey," The British Museum. https://www.britishmuseum.org/research/research_projects/all_current_projects/domuztepe_excavations_project.aspx

Tucker, Gene M. "The Legal Background of Genesis 23." *Journal of Biblical Literature* 85, no. 1 (1966): 77-84. doi:10.2307/3264358.

"Ugarit (Ras Shamra)." HOMS Online. http://www.homsonline.com/EN/Citeis/Ugarit.htm

"UN urges action against advancing deserts." Reuters. August 17, 2010. https://www.reuters.com/article/ozatp-deserts-unep-idAFJOE67G02O20100817

"Ur meaning." Abarim Publications. http://www.abarim-publications.com/Meaning/Ur.html#.XH86KYhKjIU

"War Scrolls." Qumran.org 2019. https://www.qumran.org/js/qumran/hss/1qm

Wayne, Alexander, M. "Trade And Traders Of Mesopotamian Ur," Minnesota State University Moorhead Proceedings of ASBBS Volume 19 Number 1, February 2012. http://asbbs.org/files/ASBBS2012V1/PDF/A/AlexanderW.pdf

Weiss, H., deLillis, F., deMoulins, D., Eidem, J., Guilderson, T., Kasten, U., Larsen, T., Mori, L., Ristvet, L., Rova, E., & Wetterstrom, W. . "Revising the Contours of History at Tell Leilan." *Annales Archéologiques Arabes Syriennes*, 45 59-74. 2002.Retrieved from https://repository.upenn.edu/anthro_papers/28

Westbrook, Raymond. "Slave and Master in Ancient Near Eastern Law," *Chicago-Kent Law Review* Volume 70 Issue 4 Article 12 June 1995.

"What To Do If You Know Someone Is in Trouble," YouTube video, posted by Renner Ministries, Jul 22, 2019, https://www.youtube.com/

watch?v=WwZk4Dzv8kM

Wiener, Noah. "Early Bronze Age: Megiddo's Great Temple and the Birth of Urban Culture in the Levant." Biblical Archaeology. April 8, 2018. https://www.biblicalarchaeology.org/daily/ancient-cultures/ancient-israel/early-bronze-age-megiddos-great-temple-and-the-birth-of-urban-culture-in-the-levant/

Wikipedia contributors, "Amarna letter EA 287," Wikipedia, The Free Encyclopedia, https://en.wikipedia.org/w/index.php?title=Amarna_letter_EA_287&oldid=897401136 (accessed May 30, 2019).
_____ "Saint George," Wikipedia, The Free Encyclopedia, https://en.wikipedia.org/w/index.php?title=Saint_George&oldid=912694631 (accessed August 29, 2019).
_____ "Theophilus Pinches," Wikipedia, The Free Encyclopedia, https://en.wikipedia.org/w/index.php?title=Theophilus_Pinches&oldid=745819735 (accessed May 24, 2019).
_____Urfa," Wikipedia, The Free Encyclopedia, https://en.wikipedia.org/w/index.php?title=Urfa&oldid=910518151 (accessed August 29, 2019).

Wilford, John Noble. "Camels Had No Business in Genesis," *The New York Times* Feb. 10, 2014.
_____ "At Ur, Ritual Deaths That Were Anything but Serene," *The New York Times* Oct. 26, 2009.
_____"Lost Capital of a Fabled Kingdom Found in Syria," *The New York Times.* Nov. 21, 1995.

Williams, Henry Smith. "Old Babylonian History," in *The Historians' History of the World: A Comprehensive Narrative of the Rise and Development of Nations from the Earliest Times, Volumes 1-2* (Encyclopaedia Britannica, 1907) 359-365 Google Books.

Wilson, Clifford, M.A., B.D., PH.D. "Ebla: Its Impact on Bible Records." Institute For Creation Research, April 1, 1977 https://www.icr.org/article/ebla-its-impact-bible-records/

Wilson, Dr. Ralph F. "Abraham Rescues His Nephew Lot (Genesis 13-14)." Jesuswalk.com http://www.jesuswalk.com/abraham/3_rescue.htm

Wood, Bryant G. PhD. "Great Discoveries in Biblical Archaeology: The Mari Archive." Associates for Biblical Research. February 06, 2006. http://www.biblearchaeology.org/post/2006/02/06/Great-Discoveries-in-Biblical-Archaeology-The-Mari-Archive.aspx
___ "Great Discoveries in Biblical Archaeology: The Nuzi Tablets." Associates For Biblical Research. February 27, 2006 https://biblearchaeology.org/research/patriarchal-era/3492-great-discoveries-in-biblical-archaeology-the-nuzi-tablets
___ "Hittites and Hethites: A Proposed Solution to an Etymological Conundrum." Associates For Biblical Research. November 8, 2011. https://biblearchaeology.org/research/divided-kingdom/2796-hittites-and-hethites-a-proposed-solution-to-an-etymological-conundrum
___ "Locating Sodom: A Critique of the Northern Proposal." Associates for Biblical Research. February 26,2016.
___ "Sodom and Gomorrah: Is There Evidence for Their Destruction?" Associates For Biblical Research. May 6, 2008. https://biblearchaeology.org/research/patriarchal-era/3875-sodom-and-gomorrah-is-there-evidence-for-their-destruction
___ "The Discovery of the Sin Cities of Sodom and Gomorrah." Associates For Biblical Research. April 16, 2008. http://www.biblearchaeology.org/post/2008/04/16/The-Discovery-of-the-Sin-Cities-of-Sodom-and-Gomorrah.aspx

Yener, K. Aslihan, Christopher Edens, Timothy P. Harrison, J. Verstraete, and Tony J. Wilkinson. "The Amuq Valley Regional Project, 1995-1998." *American Journal of Archaeology* 104, no. 2 (2000): 163-220. doi:10.2307/507449. https://www.jstor.org/stable/507449?read-now=1&seq=1#page_scan_tab_contents

Zettler, Richard L. "Treasures From The Royal Tombs Of Ur Ur of the Chaldees," The Oriental Institute The University of Chicago

1998. https://oi.uchicago.edu/museum-exhibits/special-exhibits/treasures-royal-tombs-ur-0

Zieve, Tamara. "Will Israel Ever Accept Messianic Jews?" *Jerusalem Post* December 16, 2017.

Zonszein, Mairav. "Domesticated Camels Came to Israel in 930 B.C., Centuries Later Than Bible Says." *National Geographic* February 10, 2014 https://news.nationalgeographic.com/news/2014/02/140210-domesticated-camels-israel-bible-archaeology-science/

www.ingramcontent.com/pod-product-compliance
Lightning Source LLC
Chambersburg PA
CBHW071340080526
44587CB00017B/2906